Chastelard by Algernon Charles Swinburne

A TRAGEDY

Algernon Charles Swinburne was born on April 5th, 1837, in London, into a wealthy Northumbrian family.   He was educated at Eton and at Balliol College, Oxford, but did not complete a degree.

In 1860 Swinburne published two verse dramas but achieved his first literary success in 1865 with Atalanta in Calydon, written in the form of classical Greek tragedy. The following year "Poems and Ballads" brought him instant notoriety. He was now identified with "indecent" themes and the precept of art for art's sake.

Although he produced much after this success in general his popularity and critical reputation declined. The most important qualities of Swinburne's work are an intense lyricism, his intricately extended and evocative imagery, metrical virtuosity, rich use of assonance and alliteration, and bold, complex rhythms.

Swinburne's physical appearance was small, frail, and plagued by several other oddities of physique and temperament. Throughout the 1860s and 1870s he drank excessively and was prone to accidents that often left him bruised, bloody, or unconscious. Until his forties he suffered intermittent physical collapses that necessitated removal to his parents' home while he recovered.

Throughout his career Swinburne also published literary criticism of great worth. His deep knowledge of world literatures contributed to a critical style rich in quotation, allusion, and comparison. He is particularly noted for discerning studies of Elizabethan dramatists and of many English and French poets and novelists. As well he was a noted essayist and wrote two novels.

In 1879, Swinburne's friend and literary agent, Theodore Watts-Dunton, intervened during a time when Swinburne was dangerously ill. Watts-Dunton isolated Swinburne at a suburban home in Putney and gradually weaned him from alcohol, former companions and many other habits as well.

Much of his poetry in this period may be inferior but some individual poems are exceptional; "By the North Sea," "Evening on the Broads," "A Nympholept," "The Lake of Gaube," and "Neap-Tide."

Swinburne lived another thirty years with Watts-Dunton. He denied Swinburne's friends access to him, controlled the poet's money, and restricted his activities. It is often quoted that 'he saved the man but killed the poet'.

Swinburne died on April 10th, 1909 at the age of seventy-two.

Index of Contents

THE PERSONS
MARY STUART
MARY BEATON
MARY SEYTON
MARY CARMICHAEL
MARY HAMILTON
PIERRE DE BOSCOSEL
DE CHASTELARD
DARNLEY
MURRAY
RANDOLPH
MORTON
LINDSAY
FATHER BLACK
Guards, Burgesses, a Preacher, Citizens, &c.

Another Yle is there toward the Northe, in the See Occean, where that ben fulle cruele and ful evele Wommen of Nature: and thei han precious Stones in hire Eyen; and their ben of that kynde, that zif they beholden ony man, thei slen him anon with the beholdynge, as dothe the Basilisk.
MAUNDEVILE'S Voiage and Travaile, Ch. xxviii.

DEDICATION

I DEDICATE THIS PLAY,
AS A PARTIAL EXPRESSION OF REVERENCE
AND GRATITUDE,
TO THE CHIEF OF LIVING POETS;
TO THE FIRST DRAMATIST OF HIS AGE;
TO THE GREATEST EXILE, AND THEREFORE

TO THE GREATEST MAN OF FRANCE;
TO
VICTOR HUGO.

SCENE I.—The Upper Chamber in Holyrood.

The four **MARIES**.

MARY BEATON (sings):—
1.
Le navire
Est a l'eau;
Entends rire
Ce gros flot
Que fait luire
Et bruire
Le vieux sire
Aquilo.

2.
Dans l'espace
Du grand air
Le vent passe
Comme un fer;
Siffle et sonne,
Tombe et tonne,
Prend et donne
A la mer.

3.
Vois, la brise
Tourne au nord,
Et la bise
Souffle et mord
Sur ta pure
Chevelure
Qui murmure
Et se tord.

MARY HAMILTON
You never sing now but it makes you sad;
Why do you sing?

MARY BEATON
I hardly know well why;

It makes me sad to sing, and very sad
To hold my peace.

MARY CARMICHAEL
I know what saddens you.

MARY BEATON
Prithee, what? what?

MARY CARMICHAEL
Why, since we came from France,
You have no lover to make stuff for songs.

MARY BEATON
You are wise; for there my pain begins indeed,
Because I have no lovers out of France.

MARY SEYTON
I mind me of one Olivier de Pesme,
(You knew him, sweet,) a pale man with short hair,
Wore tied at sleeve the Beaton color.

MARY CARMICHAEL
Blue—
I know, blue scarfs. I never liked that knight.

MARY HAMILTON
Me? I know him? I hardly knew his name.
Black, was his hair? no, brown.

MARY SEYTON
Light pleases you:
I have seen the time brown served you well enough.

MARY CARMICHAEL
Lord Darnley's is a mere maid's yellow.

MARY HAMILTON
No,
A man's, good color.

MARY SEYTON
Ah, does that burn your blood?
Why, what a bitter color is this read
That fills your face! if you be not in love,
I am no maiden.

MARY HAMILTON

Nay, God help true hearts!
I must be stabbed with love then, to the bone,
Yea to the spirit, past cure.

MARY SEYTON

What were you saying?
I see some jest run up and down your lips.

MARY CARMICHAEL

Finish your song; I know you have more of it;
Good sweet, I pray you do.

MARY BEATON

I am too sad.

MARY CARMICHAEL

This will not sadden you to sing; your song
Tastes sharp of sea and the sea's bitterness,
But small pain sticks on it.

MARY BEATON

Nay, it is sad;
For either sorrow with the beaten lips
Sings not at all, or if it does get breath
Sings quick and sharp like a hard sort of mirth:
And so this song does; or I would it did,
That it might please me better than it does.

MARY SEYTON

Well, as you choose then. What a sort of men
Crowd all about the squares!

MARY CARMICHAEL

Ay, hateful men;
For look how many talking mouths be there,
So many angers show their teeth at us.
Which one is that, stooped somewhat in the neck,
That walks so with his chin against the wind,
Lips sideways shut? a keen-faced man—lo there,
He that walks midmost.

MARY SEYTON

That is Master Knox.
He carries all these folk within his skin,
Bound up as 't were between the brows of him
Like a bad thought; their hearts beat inside his;
They gather at his lips like flies in the sun,
Thrust sides to catch his face.

MARY CARMICHAEL
Look forth; so—push
The window—further—see you anything?

MARY HAMILTON
They are well gone; but pull the lattice in,
The wind is like a blade aslant. Would God
I could get back one day I think upon:
The day we four and some six after us
Sat in that Louvre garden and plucked fruits
To cast love-lots with in the gathered grapes;
This way: you shut your eyes and reach and pluck,
And catch a lover for each grape you get.
I got but one, a green one, and it broke
Between my fingers and it ran down through them.

MARY SEYTON
Ay, and the queen fell in a little wrath
Because she got so many, and tore off
Some of them she had plucked unwittingly—
She said, against her will. What fell to you?

MARY BEATON
Me? nothing but the stalk of a stripped bunch
With clammy grape-juice leavings at the tip.

MARY CARMICHAEL
Ay, true, the queen came first and she won all;
It was her bunch we took to cheat you with.
What, will you weep for that now? for you seem
As one that means to weep. God pardon me!
I think your throat is choking up with tears.
You are not well, sweet, for a lying jest
To shake you thus much.

MARY BEATON
I am well enough:
Give not your pity trouble for my sake.

MARY SEYTON
If you be well sing out your song and laugh,
Though it were but to fret the fellows there.—
Now shall we catch her secret washed and wet
In the middle of her song; for she must weep
If she sing through.

MARY HAMILTON

I told you it was love;
I watched her eyes all through the masquing time
Feed on his face by morsels; she must weep.

MARY BEATON [sings]
4.
Le navire
Passe et luit,
Puis chavire
A grand bruit;
Et sur l'onde
La plus blonde
Tete au monde
Flotte et fuit.

5.
Moi, je rame,
Et l'amour,
C'est ma flamme,
Mon grand jour,
Ma chandelle
Blanche et belle,
Ma chapelle
De sejour.

6.
Toi, mon ame
Et ma foi,
Sois, ma dame;
Et ma loi;
Sois ma mie,
Sois Marie,
Sois ma vie,
Toute a moi!

MARY SEYTON
I know the song; a song of Chastelard's,
He made in coming over with the queen.
How hard it rained! he played that over twice
Sitting before her, singing each word soft,
As if he loved the least she listened to.

MARY HAMILTON
No marvel if he loved it for her sake;
She is the choice of women in the world;
Is she not, sweet?

MARY BEATON

I have seen no fairer one.

MARY SEYTON

And the most loving: did you note last night
How long she held him with her hands and eyes,
Looking a little sadly, and at last
Kissed him below the chin and parted so
As the dance ended?

MARY HAMILTON

This was courtesy;
So might I kiss my singing-bird's red bill
After some song, till he bit short my lip.

MARY SEYTON

But if a lady hold her bird anights
To sing to her between her fingers—ha?
I have seen such birds.

MARY CARMICHAEL

O, you talk emptily;
She is full of grace; and marriage in good time
Will wash the fool called scandal off men's lips.

MARY HAMILTON

I know not that; I know how folk would gibe
If one of us pushed courtesy so far.
She has always loved love's fashions well; you wot,
The marshal, head friend of this Chastelard's,
She used to talk with ere he brought her here
And sow their talk with little kisses thick
As roses in rose-harvest. For myself,
I cannot see which side of her that lurks,
Which snares in such wise all the sense of men;
What special beauty, subtle as man's eye
And tender as the inside of the eyelid is,
There grows about her.

MARY CARMICHAEL

I think her cunning speech—
The soft and rapid shudder of her breath
In talking—the rare tender little laugh—
The pitiful sweet sound like a bird's sigh
When her voice breaks; her talking does it all.

MARY SEYTON

I say, her eyes with those clear perfect brows:
It is the playing of those eyelashes,

The lure of amorous looks as sad as love,
Plucks all souls toward her like a net.

MARY HAMILTON
What, what!
You praise her in too lover-like a wise
For women that praise women; such report
Is like robes worn the rough side next the skin,
Frets where it warms.

MARY SEYTON
You think too much in French.

[Enter **DARNLEY**

Here comes your thorn; what glove against it now?

MARY HAMILTON
O, God's good pity! this a thorn of mine?
It has not run deep in yet.

MARY CARMICHAEL
I am not sure:
The red runs over to your face's edge.

DARNLEY
Give me one word; nay, lady, for love's sake;
Here, come this way; I will not keep you; no.
—O my sweet soul, why do you wrong me thus?

MARY HAMILTON
Why will you give me for men's eyes to burn?

DARNLEY
What, sweet, I love you as mine own soul loves me;
They shall divide when we do.

MARY HAMILTON
I cannot say.

DARNLEY
Why, look you, I am broken with the queen;
This is the rancor and the bitter heart
That grows in you; by God it is nought else.
Why, this last night she held me for a fool—
Ay, God wot, for a thing of stripe and bell.
I bade her make me marshal in her masque—
I had the dress here painted, gold and gray

(That is, not gray but a blue-green like this)—
She tells me she had chosen her marshal, she,
The best o' the world for cunning and sweet wit;
And what sweet fool but her sweet knight, God help!
To serve her with that three-inch wit of his?
She is all fool and fiddling now; for me,
I am well-pleased; God knows, if I might choose
I would not be more troubled with her love.
Her love is like a briar that rasps the flesh,
And yours is soft like flowers. Come this way, love;
So, further in this window; hark you here.

[Enter **CHASTELARD**

MARY BEATON
Good morrow, sir.

CHASTELARD
Good morrow, noble lady.

MARY CARMICHAEL
You have heard no news? what news?

CHASTELARD
Nay, I have none.
That maiden-tongued male-faced Elizabeth
Hath eyes unlike our queen's, hair not so soft,
And lips no kiss of love's could bring to flower
In such red wise as our queen's; save this news,
I know none English.

MARY SEYTON
Come, no news of her;
For God's love talk still rather of our queen.

MARY BEATON
God give us grace then to speak well of her.
You did right joyfully in our masque last night'
I saw you when the queen lost breath (her head
Bent back, her chin and lips catching the air—
A goodly thing to see her) how you smiled
Across her head, between your lips—no doubt
You had great joy, sir. Did you not take note
Once how one lock fell? that was good to see.

CHASTELARD
Yea, good enough to live for.

MARY BEATON
Nay, but sweet
Enough to die. When she broke off the dance,
Turning round short and soft—I never saw
Such supple ways of walking as she has.

CHASTLELARD
Why do you praise her gracious looks to me?

MARY BEATON
Sir, for mere sport: but tell me even for love
How much you love her.

CHASTELARD
I know not: it may be
If I had set mine eyes to find that out,
I should not know it. She hath fair eyes: may be
I love her for sweet eyes or brows or hair,
For the smooth temples, where God touching her
Made blue with sweeter veins the flower-sweet white
Or for the tender turning of her wrist,
Or marriage of the eyelid with the cheek;
I cannot tell; or flush of lifting throat,
I know not if the color get a name
This side of heaven—no man knows; or her mouth,
A flower's lip with a snake's lip, stinging sweet,
And sweet to sting with: face that one would see
And then fall blind and die with sight of it
Held fast between the eyelids—oh, all these
And all her body and the soul to that,
The speech and shape and hand and foot and heart
That I would die of—yea, her name that turns
My face to fire being written—I know no whit
How much I love them.

MARY BEATON
Nor how she loves you back?

CHASTELARD
I know her ways of loving, all of them:
A sweet soft way the first is; afterward
It burns and bites like fire; the end of that,
Charred dust, and eyelids bitten through with smoke.

MARY BEATON
What has she done for you to gird at her?

CHASTELARD

Nothing. You do not greatly love her, you,
Who do not—gird, you call it. I am bound to France;
Shall I take word from you to any one?
So it be harmless, not a gird, I will.

MARY BEATON
I doubt you will not go hence with your life.

CHASTELARD
Why, who should slay me? No man northwards born,
In my poor mind; my sword's lip is no maid's
To fear the iron biting of their own,
Though they kiss hard for hate's sake.

MARY BEATON
Lo you, sir,
How sharp he whispers, what close breath and eyes—
And here are fast upon him, do you see?

CHASTELARD
Well, which of these must take my life in hand?
Pray God it be the better: nay, which hand?

MARY BEATON
I think, none such. The man is goodly made;
She is tender-hearted toward his courtesies,
And would not have them fall too low to find.
Look, they slip forth.

[Exeunt **DARNLEY** and **MARY HAMILTON**]

MARY SEYTON
For love's sake, after them,
And soft as love can.

[Exeunt **MARY CARMICHAEL** and **MARY SEYTON**]

CHASTELARD
True, a goodly man.
What shapeliness and state he hath, what eyes,
Brave brow and lordly lip! Were it not fit
Great queens should love him?

MARY BEATON
See how now, fair lord,
I have but scant breath's time to help myself,
And I must cast my heart out on a chance;
So bear with me. That we twain have loved well,

I have no heart nor wit to say; God wot
We had never made good lovers, you and I.
Look you, I would not have you love me, sir,
For all the love's sake in the world. I say,
You love the queen, and loving burns you up,
And mars the grace and joyous wit you had,
Turning your speech to sad, your face to strange,
Your mirth to nothing: and I am piteous, I,
Even as the queen is, and such women are;
And if I helped you to your love-longing,
Meseems some grain of love might fall my way
And love's god help me when I came to love;
I have read tales of men that won their loves
On some such wise.

CHASTELARD
If you mean mercifully,
I am bound to you past thought and thank; if worse
I will but thank your lips and not your heart.

MARY BEATON
Nay, let love wait and praise me, in God's name,
Some day when he shall find me; yet, God wot,
My lips are of one color with my heart.
Withdraw now from me, and about midnight
In some close chamber without light or noise
It may be I shall get you speech of her:
She loves you well: it may be she will speak,
I wot not what; she loves you at her heart.
Let her not see that I have given you word,
Lest she take shame and hate her love. Till night
Let her not see it.

CHASTLELARD
I will not thank you now,
And then I'll die what sort of death you will.
Farewell.

[Exit.]

MARY BEATON
And by God's mercy and my love's
I will find ways to earn such thank of you.

[Exit.]

The **QUEEN, DARNLEY, MURRAY, RANDOLPH**, the **MARIES, CHASTELARD**, &c.

QUEEN
Hath no man seen my lord of Chastelard?
Nay, no great matter. Keep you on that side:
Begin the purpose.

MARY CARMICHAEL
Madam, he is here.

QUEEN
Begin a measure now that other side.
I will not dance; let them play soft a little.
Fair sir, we had a dance to tread to-night,
To teach our north folk all sweet ways of France,
But at this time we have no heart to it.
Sit, sir, and talk. Look, this breast-clasp is new,
The French king sent it me.

CHASTELARD
A goodly thing:
But what device? the word is ill to catch.

QUEEN
A Venus crowned, that eats the hearts of men:
Below her flies a love with a bat's wings,
And strings the hair of paramours to bind
Live birds' feet with. Lo what small subtle work:
The smith's name, Gian Grisostomo da—what?
Can you read that? The sea froths underfoot;
She stands upon the sea and it curls up
In soft loose curls that run to one in the wind.
But her hair is not shaken, there 's a fault;
It lies straight down in close-cut points and tongues,
Not like blown hair. The legend is writ small:
Still one makes out this—Cave—if you look.

CHASTELARD
I see the Venus well enough, God wot,
But nothing of the legend.

QUEEN
Come, fair lord,
Shall we dance now? My heart is good again.

[They dance a measure.]

DARNLEY

I do not like this manner of a dance,
This game of two by two; it were much better
To meet between the changes and to mix
Than still to keep apart and whispering
Each lady out of earshot with her friend.

MARY BEATON

That 's as the lady serves her knight, I think:
We are broken up too much.

DARNLEY

Nay, no such thing;
Be not wroth, lady, I wot it was the queen
Pricked each his friend out. Look you now—your ear—
If love had gone by choosing—how they laugh,
Lean lips together, and wring hands underhand!
What, you look white too, sick of heart, ashamed,
No marvel—for men call it—hark you though—

[They pass.]

MURRAY

Was the queen found no merrier in France?

MARY HAMILTON

Why, have you seen her sorrowful to-night?

MURRAY

I say not so much; blithe she seems at whiles,
Gentle and goodly doubtless in all ways,
But hardly with such lightness and quick heart
As it was said.

MARY HAMILTON

'Tis your great care of her
Makes you misdoubt; nought else.

MURRAY

Yea, may be so;
She has no cause I know to sadden her.

[They pass.]

QUEEN

I am tired too soon; I could have danced down hours
Two years gone hence and felt no wearier.

One grows much older northwards, my fair lord;
I wonder men die south; meseems all France
Smells sweet with living, and bright breath of days
That keep men far from dying. Peace; pray you now,
No dancing more. Sing, sweet, and make us mirth;
We have done with dancing measures: sing that song
You call the song of love at ebb.

MARY BEATON [Sings.]
1.
Between the sunset and the sea
My love laid hands and lips on me;
Of sweet came sour, of day came night,
Of long desire came brief delight:
Ah love, and what thing came of thee
Between the sea-downs and the sea?

2.
Between the sea-mark and the sea
Joy grew to grief, grief grew to me;
Love turned to tears, and tears to fire,
And dead delight to new desire;
Love's talk, love's touch there seemed to be
Between the sea-sand and the sea.

3.
Between the sundown and the sea
Love watched one hour of love with me;
Then down the all-golden water-ways
His feet flew after yesterday's;
I saw them come and saw them flee
Between the sea-foam and the sea.

4.
Between the sea-strand and the sea
Love fell on sleep, sleep fell on me;
The first star saw twain turn to one
Between the moonrise and the sun;
The next, that saw not love, saw me
Between the sea-banks and the sea.

QUEEN
Lo, sirs,
What mirth is here! Some song of yours, fair lord;
You know glad ways of rhyming—no such tunes
As go to tears.

CHASTELARD

I made this yesterday;
For its love's sake I pray you let it live.

1.

Apres tant de jours, apres tant de pleurs,
Soyez secourable a mon ame en peine.
Voyez comme Avril fait l'amour aux fleurs;
Dame d'amour, dame aux belles couleurs,
Dieu vous a fait belle, Amour vous fait reine.

2.

Rions, je t'en prie; aimons, je le veux.
Le temps fuit et rit et ne revient guere
Pour baiser le bout de tes blonds cheveux,
Pour baiser tes cils, ta bouche et tes yeux;
L'amour n'a qu'un jour aupres de sa mere.

QUEEN

'T is a true song; love shall not pluck time back
Nor time lie down with love. For me, I am old;
Have you no hair changed since you changed to Scot?
I look each day to see my face drawn up
About the eyes, as if they sucked the cheeks.
I think this air and face of things here north
Puts snow at flower-time in the blood, and tears
Between the sad eyes and the merry mouth
In their youth-days.

CHASTELARD

It is a bitter air.

QUEEN

Faith, if I might be gone, sir, would I stay?
I think, for no man's love's sake.

CHASTELARD

I think not.

QUEEN

Do you yet mind at landing how the quay
Looked like a blind wet face in waste of wind
And washing of wan waves? how the hard mist
Made the hills ache? your songs lied loud, my knight,
They said my face would burn off cloud and rain
Seen once, and fill the crannied land with fire,
Kindle the capes in their blind black-gray hoods—
I know not what. You praise me past all loves;
And these men love me little; 't is some fault,

I think, to love me: even a fool's sweet fault.
I have your verse still beating in my head
Of how the swallow got a wing broken
In the spring time, and lay upon his side
Watching the rest fly off i' the red leaf-time,
And broke his heart with grieving at himself
Before the snow came. Do you know that lord
With sharp-set eyes? and him with huge thewed throat?
Good friends to me; I had need love them well.
Why do you look one way? I will not have you
Keep your eyes here: 't is no great wit in me
To care much now for old French friends of mine.—
Come, a fresh measure; come, play well for me,
Fair sirs, your playing puts life in foot and heart.—

DARNLEY
Lo you again, sirs, how she laughs and leans,
Holding him fast—the supple way she hath!
Your queen hath none such; better as she is
For all her measures, a grave English maid,
Than queen of snakes and Scots.

RANDOLPH.
She is over fair
To be so sweet and hurt not. A good knight;
Goodly to look on.

MURRAY
Yea, a good sword too,
And of good kin; too light of loving though;
These jangling song-smiths are keen love-mongers,
They snap at all meats.

DARNLEY
What! by God I think,
For all his soft French face and bright boy's sword,
There be folks fairer: and for knightliness,
These hot-lipped brawls of Paris breed sweet knights—
Mere stabbers for a laugh across the wine.—

QUEEN
There, I have danced you down for once, fair lord;
You look pale now. Nay then for courtesy
I must needs help you; do not bow your head,
I am tall enough to reach close under it.

[Kisses him.]

Now come, we'll sit and see this passage through.—

DARNLEY

A courtesy, God help us! courtesy—
Pray God it wound not where it should heal wounds.
Why, there was here last year some lord of France
(Priest on the wrong side as some folk are prince)
Told tales of Paris ladies—nay, by God,
No jest for queen's lips to catch laughter of
That would keep clean; I wot he made good mirth,
But she laughed over sweetly, and in such wise—
But she laughed over sweetly, and in such wise—
Nay, I laughed too, but lothly.—

QUEEN

How they look!
The least thing courteous galls them to the bone.
What would one say now I were thinking of?

CHASTELARD

It seems, some sweet thing.

QUEEN

True, a sweet one, sir—
That madrigal you made Alys de Saulx
Of the three ways of love: the first kiss honor,
The second pity, and the last kiss love.
Which think you now was that I kissed you with?

CHASTELARD

It should be pity, if you be pitiful;
For I am past all honoring that keep
Outside the eye of battle, where my kin
Fallen overseas have found this many a day
No helm of mine between them; and for love,
I think of that as dead men of good days
Ere the wrong side of death was theirs, when God
Was friends with them.

QUEEN

Good; call it pity then.
You have a subtle riddling skill at love
Which is not like a lover. For my part,
I am resolved to be well done with love,
Though I were fairer-faced than all the world;
As there be fairer. Think you, fair my knight,
Love shall live after life in any man?
I have given you stuff for riddles.

CHASTELARD

Most sweet queen,
They say men dying remember, with sharp joy
And rapid reluctation of desire,
Some old thin, some swift breath of wind, some word,
Some sword-stroke or dead lute-strain, some lost sight,
Some sea-blossom stripped to the sun and burned
At naked ebb—some river-flower that breathes
Against the stream like a swooned swimmer's mouth—
Some tear or laugh ere lip and eye were man's—
Sweet stings that struck the blood in riding—nay,
Some garment or sky-color or spice-smell,
And die with heart and face shut fast on it,
And know not why, and weep not; it may be
Men shall hold love fast always in such wise
In new fair lives where all are new things else,
And know not why, and weep not.

QUEEN

A right rhyme,
And right a thyme's worth: nay, a sweet song, though.
What, shall my cousin hold fast that love of his,
Her face and talk, when life ends? as God grant
His life end late and sweet; I love him well.
She is fair enough, his lover; a fair-faced maid,
With gray sweet eyes and tender touch of talk;
And that, God wot, I wist not. See you, sir,
Men say I needs must get wed hastily;
Do none point lips at him?

CHASTELARD

Yea, guessingly.

QUEEN

God help such lips! and get me leave to laugh!
What should I do but paint and put him up
Like a gilt god, a saintship in a shrine,
For all fools' feast? God's mercy on men's wits!
Tall as a housetop and as bare of brain—
I'll have no staffs with fool-faced carven heads
To hang my life on. Nay, for love, no more,
For fear I laugh and set their eyes on edge
To find out why I laugh. Good-night, fair lords;
Bid them cease playing. Give me your hand; good-night.

Enter **CHASTELARD**

CHASTELARD
I am not certain yet she will not come;
For I can feel her hand's heat still in mine,
Past doubting of, and see her brows half draw,
And half a light in the eyes. If she come not,
I am no worse than he that dies to-night.
This two years' patience gets an end at least,
Whichever way I am well done with it.
How hard the thin sweet moon is, split and laced
And latticed over, just a stray of it
Catching and clinging at a strip of wall,
Hardly a hand's breadth. Did she turn indeed
In going out? not to catch up her gown
The page let slip, but to keep sight of me?
There was a soft small stir beneath her eyes
Hard to put on, a quivering of her blood
That knew of the old nights watched out wakefully.
Those measures of her dancing too were changed—
More swift and with more eager stops at whiles
And rapid pauses where breath failed her lips.

[Enter **MARY BEATON**]

O, she is come: if you be she indeed
Let me but hold your hand; what, no word yet?
You turn and kiss me without word; O sweet,
If you will slay me be not over quick,
Kill me with some slow heavy kiss that plucks
The heart out at the lips. Alas! Sweet love,
Give me some old sweet word to kiss away.
Is it a jest? for I can feel your hair
Touch me—I may embrace your body too?
I know you well enough without sweet words.
How should one make you speak? This is not she.
Come in the light; nay, let me see your eyes.
Ah, you it is? what have I done to you?
And do you look now to be slain for this
That you twist back and shudder like one stabbed?

MARY BEATON
Yea, kill me now and do not look at me:
God knows I meant to die. Sir, for God's love,
Kill me now quick ere I go mad with shame.

CHASTELARD

Cling not upon my wrists: let go the hilt:
Nay, you will bruise your hand with it: stand up:
You shall not have my sword forth.

MARY BEATON

Kill me now,
I will not rise: there, I am patient, see,
I will not strive, but kill me for God's sake.

CHASTELARD

Pray you rise up and be not shaken so:
Forgive me my rash words, my heart was gone
After the thing you were: be not ashamed;
Give me the shame, you have no part in it;
Can I not say a word shall do you good?
Forgive that too.

MARY BEATON

I shall run crazed with shame;
But when I felt your lips catch hold on mine
It stopped my breath: I would have told you all;
Let me go out: you see I lied to you,
Am I am shamed; I pray you loose me, sir,
Let me go out.

CHASTELARD

Think no base things of me:
I were most base to let you go ashamed.
Think my heart's love and honor go with you:
Yea, while I live, for your love's noble sake,
I am your servant in what wise may be,
To love and serve you with right thankful heart.

MARY BEATON

I have given men leave to mock me, and must bear
What shame they please: you have good cause to mock.
Let me pass now.

CHASTELARD

You know I mock you not.
If ever I leave off to honor you,
God give me shame! I were the worst churl born.

MARY BEATON

No marvel though the queen should love you too,
Being such a knight. I pray you for her love,
Lord Chastelard, of your great courtesy,

Think now no scorn to give me my last kiss
That I shall have of man before I die.
Even the same lips you kissed and knew not of
Will you kiss now, knowing the shame of them,
And say no one word to me afterwards,
That I may see I have loved the best lover
And man most courteous of all men alive?

MARY SEYTON [Within.]
Here, fetch the light: nay, this way; enter all.

MARY BEATON
I am twice undone. Fly, get some hiding, sir;
They have spied upon me somehow.

CHASTELARD
Nay, fear not;
Stand by my side.

[Enter **MARY SEYTON** and **MARY HAMILTON**]

MARY HAMILTON
Give me that light: this way.

CHASTELARD
What jest is here, fair ladies? it walks late,
Something too late for laughing.

MARY SEYTON
Nay, fair sir,
What jest is this of yours? Look to your lady:
She is nigh swooned. The queen shall know all this.

MARY HAMILTON
A grievous shame it is we are fallen upon;
Hold forth the light. Is this your care of us?
Nay, come, look up: this is no game, God wot.

CHASTELARD
Shame shall befall them that speak shamefully:
I swear this lady is as pure and good
As any maiden, and who believes me not
Shall keep the shame for his part and the lie.
To them that come in honor and not in hate
I will make answer. Lady, have good heart.
Give me the light there: I will see you forth.

SCENE I.—The Great Chamber in Holyrood.

The **QUEEN** and **MARY SEYTON**

QUEEN
But will you swear it?

MARY SEYTON
Swear it, madam?

QUEEN
Ay—
Swear it.

MARY SEYTON
Madam, I am not friends with them.

QUEEN
Swear then against them if you are not friends.

MARY SEYTON
Indeed I saw them kiss.

QUEEN
So lovers use—
What, their mouths close? a goodly way of love!
Or but the hands? or on her throat? Prithee—
You have sworn that.

MARY SEYTON
I say what I saw done.

QUEEN
Ay, you did see her cheeks (God smite them red!)
Kissed either side? what, they must eat strange food
Those singing lips of his?

MARY SEYTON
Sweet meat enough—
They started at my coming five yards off,
But there they were.

QUEEN
A maid may have kissed cheeks
And no shame in them—yet one would not swear.

You have sworn that. Pray God he be not mad:
A sickness in his eyes. The left side love
(I was told that) and the right courtesy.
'T is good fools' fashion. What, no more but this?
For me, God knows I am no whit wroth; not I;
But, for your fame's sake that her shame will sting,
I cannot see a way to pardon her—
For your fame's sake, lest that be prated of.

MARY SEYTON
Nay, if she were not chaste—I have not said
She was not chaste.

QUEEN
I know you are tender of her;
And your sweet word will hardly turn her sweet.

MARY SEYTON
Indeed I would fain do her any good.
Shall I not take some gracious word to her?

QUEEN
Bid her not come or wait on me to-day.

MARY SEYTON
Will you see him?

QUEEN
See—O, this Chastelard?
He doth not well to sing maids into shame;
And folk are sharp here; yet for sweet friends' sake
Assuredly I 'll see him. I am not wroth.
A goodly man, and a good sword thereto—
It may be he shall wed her. I am not wroth.

MARY SEYTON
Nay, though she bore with him, she hath no great love,
I doubt me, that way.

QUEEN
God mend all, I pray—
And keep us from all wrongdoing and wild words.
I think there is no fault men fall upon
But I could pardon. Look you, I would swear
She were no paramour for any man,
So well I love her.

MARY SEYTON

Am I to bid him in?

QUEEN
As you will, sweet. But if you held me hard
You did me grievous wrong. Doth he wait there?
Men call me over tender; I had rather so,
Than too ungracious. Father, what with you?

[Enter **FATHER BLACK**]

FATHER BLACK
God's peace and health of soul be with the queen!
And pardon be with me though I speak truth.
As I was going on peaceable men's wise
Through your good town, desiring no man harm,
A kind of shameful woman with thief's lips
Spake somewhat to me over a thrust-out chin,
Soliciting as I deemed an alms; which alms
(Remembering what was writ of Magdalen)
I gave no grudging but with pure good heart,
When lo some scurril children that lurked near,
Set there by Satan for my stumbling-stone,
Fell hooting with necks thwart and eyes asquint,
Screeched and made horns and shot out tongues at me,
As at my Lord the Jews shot out their tongues
And made their heads wag; I considering this
Took up my cross in patience and passed forth:
Nevertheless one ran between my feet
And made me totter, using speech and signs
I smart with shame to think of: then my blood
Kindled, and I was moved to smite the knave,
And the knave howled; whereat the lewd whole herd
Brake forth upon me and cast mire and stones
So that I ran sore risk of bruise or gash
If they had touched; likewise I heard men say,
(Their foul speech missed not mine ear) they cried,
"This devil's mass—priest hankers for new flesh
Like a dry hound; let him seek such at home,
Snuff and smoke out the queen's French—"

QUEEN
They said that?

FATHER BLACK
"—French paramours that breed more shames than sons
All her court through;" forgive me.

QUEEN

With my heart.
Father, you see the hatefulness of these—
They loathe us for our love. I am not moved:
What should I do being angry? By this hand
(Which is not big enough to bruise their lips),
I marvel what thing should be done with me
To make me wroth. We must have patience with us
When we seek thank of men.

FATHER BLACK
Madam, farewell;
I pray God keep you in such patient heart.

[Exit.]

QUEEN
Let him come now.

MARY SEYTON
Madam, he is at hand.

[Exit.]

[Enter **CHASTELARD**]

QUEEN
Give me that broidery frame; how, gone so soon?
No maid about? Reach me some skein of silk.
What, are you come, fair lord? Now by my life
That lives here idle, I am right glad of you;
I have slept so well and sweet since yesternight
It seems our dancing put me in glad heart.
Did you sleep well?

CHASTELARD
Yea, as a man may sleep.

QUEEN
You smile as if I jested; do not men
Sleep as we do? Had you fair dreams in the night?
For me—but I should fret you with my dreams—
I dreamed sweet things. You are good at soothsaying:
Make me a sonnet of my dream.

CHASTELARD
I will,
When I shall know it.

QUEEN

I thought I was asleep
In Paris, lying by my lord, and knew
In somewise he was well awake, and yet
I could not wake too; and I seemed to know
He hated me, and the least breath I made
Would turn somehow to slay or stifle me.
Then in brief time he rose and went away,
Saying, Let her dream, but when her dream is out
I will come back and kill her as she wakes.
And I lay sick and trembling with sore fear,
And still I knew that I was deep asleep;
And thinking I must dream now, or I die,
God send me some good dream lest I be slain,
Fell fancying one had bound my feet with cords
And bade me dance, and the first measure made
I fell upon my face and wept for pain:
And my cords broke, and I began the dance
To a bitter tune; and he that danced with me
Was clothed in black with long red lines and bars
And masked down to the lips, but by the chin
I knew you though your lips were sewn up close
With scarlet thread all dabbled wet in blood.
And then I knew the dream was not for good.
And striving with sore travail to reach up
And kiss you (you were taller in my dream)
I missed your lips and woke.

CHASTELARD

Sweet dreams, you said?
An evil dream I hold it for, sweet love.

QUEEN

You call love sweet; yea, what is bitter, then?
There's nothing broken sleep could hit upon
So bitter as the breaking down of love.
You call me sweet; I am not sweet to you,
Nor you—O, I would say not sweet to me,
And if I said so I should hardly lie.
But there have been those things between us, sir,
That men call sweet.

CHASTELARD

I know not how There is
Turns to There hath been; 't is a heavier change
Than change of flesh to dust. Yet though years change
And good things end and evil things grow great,
The old love that was, or that was dreamed about,

That sang and kissed and wept upon itself,
Laughed and ran mad with love of its own face,
That was a sweet thing.

QUEEN
Nay, I know not well.
'T is when the man is held fast underground
They say for sooth what manner of heart he had.
We are alive, and cannot be well sure
If we loved much or little: think you not
It were convenient one of us should die?

CHASTELARD
Madam, your speech is harsh to understand.

QUEEN
Why, there could come no change then; one of us
Would never need to fear our love might turn
To the sad thing that it may grow to be.
I would sometimes all things were dead asleep
That I have loved, all buried in soft beds
And sealed with dreams and visions, and each dawn
Sung to by sorrows, and all night assuaged
By short sweet kissed and by sweet long loves
For old life's sake, lest weeping overmuch
Should wake them in a strange new time, and arm
Memory's blind hand to kill forgetfulness.

CHASTELARD
Look, you dream still, and sadly.

QUEEN
Sooth, a dream;
For such things died or lied in sweet love's face,
And I forget them not, God help my wit!
I would the whole world were made up of sleep
And life not fashioned out of lies and loves.
We foolish women have such times, you know,
When we are weary or afraid or sick
For perfect nothing.

CHASTELARD [Aside.]
Now would one be fain
To know what bitter or what dangerous thing
She thinks of, softly chafing her soft lip.
She must mean evil.

QUEEN

Are you sad too, sir,
That you say nothing?

CHASTELARD
I? not sad a jot—
Though this your talk might make a blithe man sad.

QUEEN
O me! I must not let stray sorrows out;
They are ill to fledge, and if they feel blithe air
They wail and chirp untunefully. Would God
I had been a man! when I was born, men say,
My father turned his face and wept to think
I was no man.

CHASTELARD
Will you weep too?

QUEEN
In sooth,
If I were a man I should be no base man;
I could have fought; yea, I could fight now too
If men would show me; I would I were the king!
I should be all ways better than I am.

CHASTELARD
Nay, would you have more honor, having this—
Men's hearts and loves and the sweet spoil of souls
Given you like simple gold to bind your hair?
Say you were king of thews, not queen of souls,
An iron headpiece hammered to a head,
You might fall too.

QUEEN
No, then I would not fall,
Or God should make me woman back again.
To be King James—you hear men say King James,
The word sounds like a piece of gold thrown down,
Rings with a round and royal note in it—
A name to write good record of; this king
Fought here and there, was beaten such a day,
And came at last to a good end, his life
Being all lived out, and for the main part well
And like a king's life; then to have men say
(As now they say of Flodden, here they broke
And there they held up to the end) years back
They saw you—yea, I saw the king's face helmed
Red in the hot lit foreground of some fight

Hold the whole war as it were by the bit, a horse
Fit for his knees' grip—the great rearing war
That frothed with lips flung up, and shook men's lives
Off either flank of it like snow; I saw
(You could not hear as his sword rang), saw him
Shout, laugh, smite straight, and flaw the riven ranks,
Move as the wind moves, and his horse's feet
Stripe their long flags with dust. Why, if one died,
To die so in the heart and heat of war
Were a much goodlier thing than living soft
And speaking sweet for fear of men. Woe's me,
Is there no way to pluck this body off?
Then I should never fear a man again,
Even in my dreams I should not; no, by heaven.

CHASTELARD
I never thought you did fear anything.

QUEEN
God knows I do; I could be sick with wrath
To think what grievous fear I have 'twixt whiles
Of mine own self and of base men: last night
If certain lords were glancing where I was
Under the eyelid, with sharp lip and brow,
I tell you, for pure shame and fear of them,
I could have gone and slain them.

CHASTELARD
Verily,
You are changed since those good days that fell in France;
But yet I think you are not so changed at heart
As to fear man.

QUEEN
I would I had no need.
Lend me your sword a little; a fair sword;
I see the fingers that I hold it with
Clear in the blade, bright pink, the shell-color,
Brighter than flesh is really, curved all round.
Now men would mock if I should wear it here,
Bound under bosom with a girdle, here,
And yet I have heart enough to wear it well.
Speak to me like a woman, let me see
If I can play at man.

CHASTELARD
God save King James!

QUEEN

Would you could change now! Fie, this will not do;
Unclasp your sword; nay, the hilt hurts my side;
It sticks fast here. Unbind this knot for me:
Stoop, and you'll see it closer; thank you: there.
Now I can breathe, sir. Ah! it hurts me, though:
This was fool's play.

CHASTELARD

Yea, you are better so,
Without the sword; your eyes are stronger things,
Whether to save or slay.

QUEEN

Alas, my side!
It hurts right sorely. Is it not pitiful
Our souls should be so bound about with flesh
Even when they leap and smite with wings and feet,
The least pain plucks them back, puts out their eyes,
Turns them to tears and words? Ah my sweet knight,
You have the better of us that weave and weep
While the blithe battle blows upon your eyes
Like rain and wind; yet I remember too
When this last year the fight at Corrichie
Reddened the rushes with stained fen-water,
I rode with my good men and took delight,
Feeling the sweet clear wind upon my eyes
And rainy soft smells blown upon my face
In riding: then the great fight jarred and joined,
And the sound stung me right through heart and all;
For I was here, see, gazing off the hills,
In the wet air; our housings were all wet,
And not a plume stood stiffly past the ear
But flapped between the bridle and the neck;
And under us we saw the battle go
Like running water; I could see by fits
Some helm the rain fell shining off, some flag
Snap from the staff, shorn through or broken short
In the man's falling: yea, one seemed to catch
The very grasp of tumbled men at men,
Teeth clenched in throats, hands riveted in hair,
Tearing the life out with no help of swords.
And all the clamor seemed to shine, the light
Seemed to shout as a man doth; twice I laughed—
I tell you, twice my heart swelled out with thirst
To be into the battle; see, fair lord,
I swear it seemed I might have made a knight,
And yet the simple bracing of a belt

Makes me cry out; this is too pitiful,
This dusty half of us made up with fears.—
Have you been ever quite so glad to fight
As I have thought men must? pray you, speak truth.

CHASTELARD
Yea, when the time came, there caught hold of me
Such pleasure in the head and hands and blood
As may be kindled under loving lips:
Crossing the ferry once to the Clerks' Field,
I mind how the plashing noise of Seine
Put fire into my face for joy, and how
My blood kept measure with the swinging boat
Till we touched land, all for the sake of that
Which should be soon.

QUEEN
Her name, for God's love, sir;
You slew your friend for love's sake? nay, the name.

CHASTELARD
Faith, I forget.

QUEEN
Now by the faith I have
You have no faith to swear by.

CHASTELARD
A good sword:
We left him quiet after a thrust or twain.

QUEEN
I would I had been at hand and marked them off
As the maids did when we played singing games:
You outwent me at rhyming; but for faith,
We fight best there. I would I had seen you fight.

CHASTELARD
I would you had; his play was worth an eye;
He made some gallant way before that pass
Which made me way through him.

QUEEN
Would I saw that—
How did you slay him?

CHASTELARD
A clean pass—this way;

Right in the side here, where the blood has root.
His wrist went round in pushing, see you, thus,
Or he had pierced me.

QUEEN

Yea, I see, sweet knight.
I have a mind to love you for his sake;
Would I had seen.

CHASTELARD

Hugues de Marsillac—
I have the name now; 't was a goodly one
Before he changed it for a dusty name.

QUEEN

Talk not of death; I would hear living talk
Of good live swords and good strokes struck withal,
Brave battles and the mirth of mingling men,
Not of cold names you greet a dead man with.
You are yet young for fighting; but in fight
Have you never caught a wound?

CHASTELARD

Yea, twice or so:
The first time in a little outlying field
(My first field) at the sleepy gray of dawn,
They found us drowsy, fumbling at our girths,
And rode us down by heaps; I took a hurt
Here in the shoulder.

QUEEN

Ah, I mind well now;
Did you not ride a day's space afterward,
Having two wounds? yea, Dandelot it was,
That Dandelot took word of it. I know,
Sitting at meat when the news came to us
I had nigh swooned but for those Florence eyes
Slanting my way with sleek lids drawn up close—
Yea, and she said, the Italian brokeress,
She said such men were good for great queens' love.
I would you might die, when you come to die,
Like a knight slain. Pray God we make good ends.
For love too, love dies hard or easily,
But some way dies on some day, ere we die.

CHASTELARD

You made a song once of old flowers and loves,
Will you not sing that rather? 't is long gone

Since you sang last.

QUEEN
I had rather sigh than sing
And sleep than sigh; 't is long since verily,
But I will once more sing; ay, thus it was.
[Sings.]
1.
J'ai vu faner bien des choses,
Mainte feuille aller au vent.
En songeant aux vieilles roses,
J'ai pleure souvent.

2.
Vois-tu dans les roses mortes
Amour qui sourit cache?
O mon amant, a nos portes
L'as-tu vu couche?

3.
As-tu vu jamais au monde
Venus chasser et courir?
Fille de l'onde, avec l'onde
Doit-elle mourir?

4.
Aux jours de neige et de givre
L'amour s'effeuille et s'endort;
Avec mai doit-il revivre,
Ou bien est-il mort?

5.
Qui sait ou s'en vont les roses?
Qui sai ou s'en va le vent?
En songeant a telles choses,
J'ai pleure souvent.

I never heard yet but love made good knights,
But for pure faith, by Mary's holiness,
I think she lies about men's lips asleep,
And if one kiss or pluck her by the hand
To wake her, why God help your woman's wit,
Faith is but dead; dig her grave deep at heart,
And hide her face with cerecloths; farewell faith.
Would I could tell why I talk idly. Look,
Here come my riddle-readers. Welcome all;

[Enter **MURRAY, DARNLEY, RANDOLPH, LINDSAY, MORTON,** and other **LORDS.**]

Sirs, be right welcome. Stand you by my side,
Fair cousin, I must lean on love or fall;
You are a goodly staff, sir; tall enough,
And fair enough to serve. My gentle lords,
I am full glad of God that in great grace
He hath given me such a lordly stay as this;
There is no better friended queen alive.
For the repealing of those banished men
That stand in peril yet of last year's fault,
It is our will; you have our seal to that.
Brother, we hear harsh bruits of bad report
Blown up and down about our almoner;
See you to this: let him be sought into:
They say lewd folk make ballads of their spleen,
Strew miry ways of words with talk of him;
If they have cause let him be spoken with.

LINDSAY

Madam, they charge him with so rank a life
Were it not well this fellow were plucked out—
Seeing this is not an eye that doth offend,
But a blurred glass it were no harm to break;
Yea rather it were gracious to be done?

QUEEN

Let him be weighed, and use him as he is;
I am of my nature pitiful, ye know,
And cannot turn my love unto a thorn
In so brief space. Ye are all most virtuous;
Yea, there is goodness grafted on this land;
But yet compassion is some part of God.
There is much heavier business held on hand
Than one man's goodness: yea, as things fare here,
A matter worth more weighing. All you wot
I am choose a help to my weak feet,
A lamp before my face, a lord and friend
To walk with me in weary ways, high up
Between the wind and rain and the hot sun.
Now I have chosen a helper to myself,
I wot the best a woman ever won;
A man that loves me, and a royal man,
A goodly love and lord for any queen.
But for the peril and despite of men
I have sometime tarried and withheld myself,
Not fearful of his worthiness nor you,
But with some lady's loathing to let out
My whole heart's love; for truly this is hard,

Not like a woman's fashion, shamefacedness
And noble grave reluctance of herself
To be the tongue and cry of her own heart.
Nathless plain speech is better than much wit,
So ye shall bear with me; albeit I think
Ye have caught the mark whereat my heart is bent.
I have kept close counsel and shut up men's lips,
But lightly shall a woman's will slip out,
The foolish little winged will of her,
Through cheek or eye when tongue is charmed asleep.
For that good lord I have good will to wed,
I wot he knew long since which way it flew,
Even till it lit on his right wrist and sang.
Lo, here I take him by the hand: fair lords,
This is my kinsman, made of mine own blood,
I take to halve the state and services
That bow down to me, and to be my head,
My chief, my master, my sweet lord and king.
Now shall I never say "sweet cousin" more
To my dear head and husband; here, fair sir,
I give you all the heart of love in me
To gather off my lips. Did it like you,
The taste of it? sir, it was whole and true.
God save our king!

DARNLEY
Nay, nay, sweet love, no lord;
No king of yours though I were lord of these.

QUEEN
Let word be sent to all good friends of ours
To help us to be glad; England and France
Shall bear great part of our rejoicings up.
Give me your hand, dear lord; for from this time
I must not walk alone. Lords, have good cheer:
For you shall have a better face than mine
To set upon your kingly gold and show
For Scotland's forehead in the van of things.
Go with us now, and see this news set out.

[Exeunt **QUEEN**, **DARNLEY**, and **LORDS**.]

[As **CHASTELARD** is going out, enter **MARY BEATON**]

MARY BEATON
Have you yet heard? You knew of this?

CHASTELARD

I know.
I was just thinking how such things were made
And were so fair as this is. Do you know
She held me here and talked—the most sweet talk
Men ever heard of?

MARY BEATON

You hate me to the heart.
What will you do?

CHASTELARD

I know not: die some day,
But live as long and lightly as I can.
Will you now love me? faith, but if you do,
It were much better you were dead and hearsed.
Will you do one thing for me?

MARY BEATON

Yea, all things.

CHASTELARD

Speak truth a little, for God's sake: indeed
It were no harm to do. Come, will you, sweet?
Though it be but to please God.

MARY BEATON

What will you do?

CHASTELARD

Ay, true, I must do somewhat. Let me see:
To get between and tread upon his face—
Catch both her hands and bid men look at them,
How pure they were—I would do none of these,
Though they got wedded all the days in the year.
We may do well yet when all's come and gone.
I pray you on this wedding-night of theirs
Do but one thing that I shall ask of you,
And Darnley will not hunger as I shall
For that good time. Sweet, will you swear me this?

MARY BEATON

Yea; though to do it were mortal to my soul
As the chief sin.

CHASTELARD

I thank you: let us go.

SCENE I.—The Queen's Chamber. Night. Lights Burning in Front of the Bed.

[Enter **CHASTELARD** and **MARY BEATON**]

MARY BEATON
Be tender of your feet.

CHASTELARD
I shall not fail:
These ways have light enough to help a man
That walks with such stirred blood in him as mine.

MARY BEATON
I would yet plead with you to save your head:
Nay, let this be then: sir, I chide you not.
Nay, let all come. Do not abide her yet.

CHASTELARD
Have you read never in French books the song
Called the Duke's Song, some boy made ages back,
A song of drag-nets hauled across thwart seas
And plucked up with rent sides, and caught therein
A strange-haired woman with sad singing lips,
Cold in the cheek like any stray of sea,
And sweet to touch? so that men seeing her face,
And how she sighed out little Ahs of pain
And soft cries sobbing sideways from her mouth,
Fell in hot love, and having lain with her
Died soon? one time I could have told it through:
Now I have kissed the sea-witch on her eyes
And my lips ache with it; but I shall sleep
Full soon, and a good space of sleep.

MARY BEATON
Alas!

CHASTELARD
What makes you sigh though I be found a fool?
You have no blame: and for my death, sweet friend,
I never could have lived long either way.
Why, as I live, the joy I have of this
Would make men mad that were not mad with love;
I hear my blood sing, and my lifted heart
Is like a springing water blown of wind
For pleasure of this deed. Now, in God's name,

I swear if there be danger in delight
I must die now: if joys have deadly teeth,
I'll have them bite my soul to death, and end
In the old asp's way, Egyptian-wise; be killed
In a royal purple fashion. Look, my love
Would kill me if my body were past hurt
Of any man's hand; and to die thereof,
I say, is sweeter than all sorts of life.
I would not have her love me now, for then
I should die meanlier some time. I am safe,
Sure of her face, my life's end in her sight,
My blood shed out about her feet—by God,
My heart feels drunken when I think of it.
See you, she will not rid herself of me,
Not though she slay me: her sweet lips and life
Will smell of my spilt blood.

MARY BEATON
Give me good-night.

CHASTELARD
Yea, and good thanks.

[Exit **MARY BEATON**]

Here is the very place:
Here has her body bowed the pillows in
And here her head thrust under made the sheet
Smell sort of her mixed hair and spice: even here
Her arms pushed back the coverlet, pulled here
The golden silken curtain halfway in
It may be, and made room to lean out loose,
Fair tender fallen arms. Now, if God would,
Doubtless he might take pity on my soul
To give me three clear hours, and then red hell
Snare me forever: this were merciful:
If I were God now I should do thus much.
I must die next, and this were not so hard
For him to let me eat sweet fruit and die
With my lips sweet from it. For one shall have
This fare for common days'-bread, which to me
Should be a touch kept always on my sense
To make hell soft, yea, the keen pain of hell
Soft as the loosening of wound arms in sleep.
Ah, love is good, and the worst part of it
More than all things but death. She will be here
In some small while, and see me face to face
That am to give up life for her and go

Where a man lies with all his loves put out
And his lips full of earth. I think on her,
And the old pleasure stings and makes half-tears
Under mine eyelids. Prithee, love, come fast,
That I may die soon: yea, some kisses through,
I shall die joyfully enough, so God
Keep me alive till then. I feel her feet
Coming far off; now must I hold my heart,
Steadying my blood to see her patiently.

[Hides himself by the bed.]

[Enter the **QUEEN** and **DARNLEY**]

QUEEN
Nay, now go back: I have sent off my folk,
Maries and all. Pray you, let be my hair;
I cannot twist the gold thread out of it
That you wound in so close. Look, here it clings:
Ah! now you mar my hair unwinding it.
Do me no hurt, sir.

DARNLEY
I would do you ease;
Let me stay here.

QUEEN
Nay, will you go, my lord?

DARNLEY
Eh? would you use me as a girl does fruit,
Touched with her mouth and pulled away for game
To look thereon ere her lips feed? but see,
By God, I fare the worse for you.

QUEEN
Fair sir,
Give me this hour to watch with and say prayers;
You have not faith—it needs me to say prayers,
That with commending of this deed to God
I may get grace for it.

DARNLEY
Why, lacks it grace?
Is not all wedlock gracious of itself?

QUEEN
Nay, that I know not of. Come, sweet, be hence.

DARNLEY
You have a sort of jewel in your neck
That's like mine here.

QUEEN
Keep off your hands and go:
You have no courtesy to be a king.

DARNLEY
Well, I will go: nay, but I thwart you not.
Do as you will, and get you grace; farewell,
And for my part, grace keep this watch with me!
For I need grace to bear with you so much.

[Exit.]

QUEEN
So, he is forth. Let me behold myself;
I am too pale to be so hot; I marvel
So little color should be bold in the face
When the blood is not quieted. I have
But a brief space to cool my thoughts upon.
If one should wear the hair thus heaped and curled
Would it look best? or this way in the neck?
Could one ungirdle in such wise one's heart

[Taking off her girdle.]

And ease it inwards as the waist is eased
By slackening of the slid clasp on it!
How soft the silk is—gracious color too;
Violet shadows like new veins thrown up
Each arm, and gold to fleck the faint sweet green
Where the wrist lies thus eased. I am right glad
I have no maids about to hasten me—
So I will rest and see my hair shed down
On either silk side of my woven sleeves,
Get some new way to bind it back with—yea,
Fair mirror-glass, I am well ware of you,
Yea, I know that, I am quite beautiful.
How my hair shines!—Fair face, be friends with me
And I will sing to you; look in my face
Now, and your mouth must help the song in mine.

Alys la chatelaine
Voit venir de par Seine
Thiebault le capitaine

Qui parle ainsi!

Was that the wind in the casement? nay, no more
But the comb drawn through half my hissing hair
Laid on my arms—yet my flesh moved at it.

Dans ma camaille
Plus de clou qui vaille,
Dans ma cotte-maille
Plus de fer aussi.

Ah, but I wrong the ballad-verse: what's good
In such frayed fringes of old rhymes, to make
Their broken burden lag with us? meseems
I could be sad now if I fell to think
The least sad thing; aye, that sweet lady's fool,
Fool sorrow, would make merry with mine eyes
For a small thing. Nay, but I will keep glad,
Nor shall old sorrow be false friends with me.
But my first wedding was not like to this—
Fair faces then and laughter and sweet game,
And a pale little mouth that clung on mine
When I had kissed him by the faded eyes
And either thin cheek beating with faint blood.
Well, he was sure to die soon; I do think
He would have given his body to be slain,
Having embraced my body. Now, God knows,
I have no man to do as much for me
As give me but a little of his blood
To fill my beauty from, though I go down
Pale to my grave for want—I think not. Pale—
I am too pale purely—Ah!

[See him in the glass, coming forward.]

CHASTELARD
Be not afraid.

QUEEN
Saint Mary! what a shaken wit have I!
Nay, is it you? who let you through the doors?
Where be my maidens? which way got you in?
Nay, but stand up, kiss not my hands so hard;
By God's fair body, if you but breathe on them
You are just dead and slain at once. What adder
Has bit you mirthful mad? for by this light
A man to have his head laughed off for mirth
Is no great jest. Lay not your eyes on me;

What, would you not be slain?

CHASTELARD
I pray you, madam,
Bear with me a brief space and let me speak.
I will not touch your garments even, nor speak
But in soft wise, and look some other way,
If that it like you; for I came not here
For pleasure of the eyes; yet, if you will,
Let me look on you.

QUEEN
As you will, fair sir.
Give me that coif to gather in my hair—
I thank you—and my girdle—nay, that side.
Speak, if you will; yet if you will be gone,
Why, you shall go, because I hate you not.
You know that I might slay you with my lips,
With calling out? but I will hold my peace.

CHASTELARD
Yea, do some while. I had a thing to say;
I know not wholly what thing. O my sweet,
I am come here to take farewell of love
That I have served, and life that I have lived
Made up of love, here in the sight of you
That all my life's time I loved more than God,
Who quits me thus with bitter death for it.
For you well know that I must shortly die,
My life being wound about you as it is,
Who love me not; yet do not hate me, sweet,
But tell me wherein I came short of love;
For doubtless I came short of a just love,
And fell in some fool's fault that angered you.
Now that I talk men dig my grave for me
Out in the rain, and in a little while
I shall be thrust in some sad space of earth
Out of your eyes; and you, O you my love,
A newly-wedded lady full of mirth
And a queen girt with all good people's love,
You shall be fair and merry in all your days.
Is this so much for me to have of you?
Do but speak, sweet: I know these are no words
A man should say though he were now to die,
But I am as a child for love, and have
No strength at heart; yea, I am afraid to die,
For the harsh dust will lie upon my face
Too thick to see you past. Look how I love you;

I did so love you always, that your face
Seen through my sleep has wrung mine eyes to tears
For pure delight in you. Why do you thus?
You answer not, but your lips curl in twain
And your face moves; there, I shall make you weep
And be a coward too; it were much best
I should be slain.

QUEEN
Yea, best such folk were slain;
Why should they live to cozen fools with lies?
You would swear now you have used me faithfully;
Shall I not make you swear? I am ware of you:
You will not do it; nay, for the fear of God
You will not swear. Come, I am merciful;
God made a foolish woman, making me,
And I have loved your mistress with whole heart;
Say you do love her, you shall marry her
And she give thanks: yet I could wish your love
Had not so lightly chosen forth a face;
For your fair sake, because I hate you not.

CHASTELARD
What is to say? why, you do surely know
That since my days were counted for a man's
I have loved you; yea, how past all help and sense,
Whatever thing was bitter to my love,
I have loved you; how when I rode in war
Your face went floated in among men's helms,
Your voice went through the shriek of slipping swords;
Yea, and I never have loved women well,
Seeing always in my sight I had your lips
Curled over, red and sweet; and the soft space
Of carven brows, and splendor of great throat
Swayed lily-wise; what pleasure should one have
To wind his arms about a lesser love?
I have seen you; why, this were joy enough
For God's eyes up in heaven, only to see
And to come never nearer than I am.
Why, it was in my flesh, my bone and blood,
Bound in my brain, to love you; yea, and writ
All my heart over: if I would lie to you
I doubt I could not lie. Ah, you see now,
You know now well enough; yea, there, sweet love,
Let me kiss there.

QUEEN
I love you best of them.

Clasp me quite round till your lips cleave on mine,
False mine, that did you wrong. Forgive them dearly
As you are sweet to them; for by love's love
I am not that evil woman in my heart
That laughs at a rent faith. O Chastelard,
Since this was broken to me of your new love
I have not seen the face of a sweet hour.
Nay, if there be no pardon in a man,
What shall a woman have for loving him?
Pardon me, sweet.

CHASTELARD
Yea, so I pardon you,
And this side now; the first way. Would God please
To slay me so! who knows how he might please?
Now I am thinking, if you know it not,
How I might kill you, kiss your breath clean out,
And take your soul to bring mine through to God,
That our two souls might close and be one twain
Or a twain one, and God himself want skill
To set us either severally apart.
O, you must overlive me many years.
And many years my soul be in waste hell;
But when some time God can no more refrain
To lay death like a kiss across your lips,
And great lords bear you clothed with funeral things,
And your crown girded over deadly brows,
Then after you shall touch me with your eyes,
Remembering love was fellow with my flesh
Here in sweet earth, and make me well of love
And heal my many years with piteousness.

QUEEN
You talk too sadly and too feignedly.

CHASTELARD
Too sad, but not too feigned; I am sad
That I shall die here without feigning thus;
And without feigning I were fain to live.

QUEEN
Alas, you will be taken presently
And then you are but dead. Pray you get hence.

CHASTELARD
I will not.

QUEEN

Nay, for God's love be away;
You will be slain and I get shame. God's mercy!
You were stark mad to come here; kiss me, sweet.
Oh, I do love you more than all men! yea,
Take my lips to you, close mine eyes up fast,
So you leave hold a little; there, for pity,
Abide now, and to-morrow come to me.
Nay, lest one see red kisses in my throat—
Dear God! what shall I give you to be gone?

CHASTELARD
I will not go. Look, here's full night grown up;
Why should I seek to sleep away from here?
The place is soft and the lights burn for sleep;
Be not you moved; I shall lie well enough.

QUEEN
You are utterly undone. Sweet, by my life,
You shall be saved with taking ship at once.
For if you stay this foolish love's hour out
There is not ten days' likely life in you.
This is no choice.

CHASTELARD
Nay, for I will not go.

QUEEN
O me! this is that Bayard's blood of yours
That makes you mad; yea, and you shall not stay.
I do not understand. Mind, you must die.
Alas, poor lord, you have no sense of me;
I shall be deadly to you.

CHASTELARD
Yea, I saw that;
But I saw not that when my death's day came
You could be quite so sweet to me.

QUEEN
My love!
If I could kiss my heart's root out on you
You would taste love hid at the core of me.

CHASTELARD
Kiss me twice more. This beautiful bowed head
That has such hair with kissing ripples in
And shivering soft eyelashes and brows
With fluttered blood! but laugh a little, sweetly,

That I may see your sad mouth's laughing look
I have used sweet hours in seeing. O, will you weep?
I pray you do not weep.

QUEEN
Nay, dear, I have
No tears in me; I never shall weep much,
I think, in all my life; I have wept for wrath
Sometimes and for mere pain, but for love's pity
I cannot weep at all. I would to God
You loved me less; I give you all I can
For all this love of yours, and yet I am sure
I shall live out the sorrow of your death
And be glad afterwards. You know I am sorry.
I should weep now; forgive me for your part,
God made me hard, I think. Alas, you see
I had fain been other than I am.

CHASTELARD
Yea, love.
Comfort your heart. What way am I do die?

QUEEN
Ah, will you go yet, sweet?

CHASTELARD
No, by God's body.
You will not see? how shall I make you see?
Look, it may be love was a sort of curse
Made for my plague and mixed up with my days
Somewise in their beginning; or indeed
A bitter birth begotten of sad stars
At mine own body's birth, that heaven might make
My life taste sharp where other men drank sweet;
But whether in heavy body or broken soul,
I know it must go on to be my death.
There was the matter of my fate in me
When I was fashioned first, and given such life
As goes with a sad end; no fault but God's.
Yea, and for all this I am not penitent:
You see I am perfect in these sins of mine,
I have my sins writ in a book to read;
Now I shall die and be well done with this.
But I am sure you cannot see such things,
God knows I blame you not.

QUEEN
What shall be said?

You know most well that I am sorrowful.
But you should chide me. Sweet, you have seen fair wars,
Have seen men slain and ridden red in them;
Why will you die a chamberer's death like this?
What, shall no praise be written of my knight,
For my fame's sake?

CHASTELARD
Nay, no great praise, I think;
I will no more; what should I do with death,
Though I died goodly out of sight of you?
I have gone once: here am I set now, sweet,
Till the end come. That is your husband, hark,
He knocks at the outer door. Kiss me just once.
You know now all you have to say. Nay, love,
Let him come quickly.

[Enter **DARNLEY**, and afterwards the **MARIES**.]

DARNLEY
Yea, what thing is here?
Ay, this was what the doors shut fast upon—
Ay, trust you to be fast at prayer, my sweet?
By God I have a mind—

CHASTELARD
What mind then, sir?
A liar's lewd mind, to coin sins for jest,
Because you take me in such wise as this?
Look you, I have to die soon, and I swear,
That am no liar but a free knight and lord,
I shall die clear of any sin to you,
Save that I came for no good will of mine;
I am no carle, I play fair games with faith,
And by mine honor for my sake I swear
I say but truth; for no man's sake save mine,
Lest I die shamed. Madam, I pray you say
I am no liar; you know me what I am,
A sinful man and shortly to be slain,
That in a simple insolence of love
Have stained with a fool's eyes your holy hours
And with a fool's words put your pity out;
Nathless you know if I be liar or no,
Wherefore for God's sake give me grace to swear
(Yea, for mine too) how past all praise you are
And stainless of all shame; and how all men
Lie, saying you are not most good and innocent,
Yea, the one thing good as God.

DARNLEY

O sir, we know
You can swear well, being taken; you fair French
Dare swallow God's name for a lewd love-sake
As it were water. Nay, we know, we know;
Save your sweet breath now lest you lack it soon:
We are simple, we; we have not heard of you.
Madam, by God you are well shamed in him:
Ay, trust you to be fingering in one's face,
Play with one's neck-chain? ah, your maiden's man,
A relic of your people's!

CHASTELARD

Hold your peace,
Or I will set an edge on your own lie
Shall scar yourself. Madam, have out your guard;
'T is time I were got hence.

QUEEN

Sweet Hamilton,
Hold you my hand and help me to sit down.
O Henry, I am beaten from my wits—
Let me have time and live; call out my people—
Bring forth some armed guard to lay hold on him:
But see no man be slain.
Sirs, hide your swords;
I will not have men slain.

DARNLEY

What, is this true?
Call the queen's people—help the queen there, you—
Ho, sirs, come in.

[Enter some with the **GUARD**.]

QUEEN

Lay hold upon that man;
Bear him away, but see he have no hurt.

CHASTELARD

Into your hands I render up myself
With a free heart; deal with me how you list,
But courteously, I pray you. Take my sword.
Farewell, great queen; the sweetness in your look
Makes life look bitter on me. Farewell, sirs.

[He is taken out.]

DARNLEY
Yea, pluck him forth, and have him hanged by dawn;
He shall find bed enow to sleep. God's love!
That such a knave should be a knight like this!

QUEEN
Sir, peace awhile; this shall be as I please;
Take patience to you. Lords, I pray you see
All be done goodly; look they wrong him not.
Carmichael, you shall sleep with me to-night;
I am sorely shaken, even to the heart. Fair lords,
I thank you for your care. Sweet, stay by me.

ACT IV - MURRAY

SCENE I.—The Queen's Lodging at St. Andrew's.

The **QUEEN** and the four **MARIES.**

QUEEN
Why will you break my heart with praying to me?
You Seyton, you Carmichael, you have wits,
You are not all run to tears; you do not think
It is my wrath or will that whets this axe
Against his neck?

MARY SEYTON
Nay, these three weeks agone
I said the queen's wrath was not sharp enough
To shear a neck.

QUEEN
Sweet, and you did me right,
And look you, what my mercy bears to fruit,
Danger and deadly speech and a fresh fault
Before the first was cool in people's lips;
A goodly mercy: and I wash hands of it.—
Speak you, there; have you ever found me sharp?
You weep and whisper with sloped necks and heads
Like two sick birds; do you think shame of me?
Nay, I thank God none can think shame of me;
But am I bitter, think you, to men's faults?
I think I am too merciful, too meek:
Why if I could I would yet save this man;
'T is just boy's madness; a soft stripe or two

Would do to scourge the fault in his French blood.
I would fain let him go. You, Hamilton,
You have a heart thewed harder than my heart;
When mine would threat it sighs, and wrath in it
Has a bird's flight and station, starves before
It can well feed or fly; my pulse of wrath
Sounds tender as the running down of tears.
You are the hardest woman I have known,
Your blood has frost and cruel gall in it,
You hold men off with bitter lips and eyes—
Such maidens should serve England; now, perfay,
I doubt you would have got him slain at once.
Come, would you not? come, would you let him live?

MARY HAMILTON
Yes—I think yes; I cannot tell; maybe
I would have seen him punished.

QUEEN
Look you now,
There's maiden mercy; I would have him live—
For all my wifehood maybe I weep too;
Here's a mere maiden falls to slaying at once,
Small shrift for her; God keep us from such hearts!
I am a queen too that would have him live,
But one that has no wrong and is no queen,
She would—What are you saying there, you twain?

MARY CARMICHAEL
I said a queen's face and so fair an one's
Would lose no grace for giving grace away;
That gift comes back upon the mouth it left
And makes it sweeter, and set fresh red on it.

QUEEN
This comes of sonnets when the dance draws breath;
These talking times will make a dearth of grace.
But you—what ails you that your lips are shut?
Weep, if you will; here are four friends of yours
To weep as fast for pity of your tears.
Do you desire him dead? nay, but men say
He was your friend, he fought them on your side,
He made you songs—God knows what songs he made!
Speak you for him a little: will you not?

MARY BEATON
Madam, I have no words.

QUEEN

No words? no pity—
Have you no mercies for such men? God help!
It seems I am the meekest heart on earth—
Yea, the one tender woman left alive,
And knew it not. I will not let him live,
For all my pity of him.

MARY BEATON

Nay, but, madam,
For God's love look a little to this thing.
If you do slay him you are but shamed to death;
All men will cry upon you, women weep,
Turning your sweet name bitter with their tears;
Red shame grow up out of your memory
And burn his face that would speak well of you:
You shall have no good word nor pity, none,
Till some such end be fallen upon you: nay,
I am but cold, I knew I had no words,
I will keep silence.

QUEEN

Yea now, as I live,
I wist not of it: troth, he shall not die.
See you, I am pitiful, compassionate,
I would not have men slain for my love's sake,
But if he live to do me three times wrong,
Why then my shame would grow up green and red
Like any flower. I am not whole at heart;
In faith, I wot not what such things should be;
I doubt it is but dangerous; he must die.

MARY BEATON

Yea, but you will not slay him.

QUEEN

Swear me that,
I'll say he shall not die for your oath's sake.
What will you do for grief when he is dead?

MARY BEATON

Nothing for grief, but hold my peace and die.

QUEEN

Why, for your sweet sake one might let him live;
But the first fault was a green seed of shame,
And now the flower, and deadly fruit will come
With apple-time in autumn. By my life,

I would they had slain him there in Edinburgh;
But I reprieve him; lo the thank I get,
To set the base folk muttering like smoked bees
Of shame and love, and how love comes to shame,
And the queen loves shame that comes of love;
Yet I say nought and go about my ways,
And this mad fellow that I respited
Being forth and free, lo now the second time
Ye take him by my bed in wait. Now see
If I can get good-will to pardon him;
With what a face may I crave leave of men
To respite him, being young and a good knight
And mad for perfect love? shall I go say,
Dear lords, because ye took him shamefully,
Let him not die; because his fault is foul,
Let him not die; because if he do live
I shall be held a harlot of all men,
I pray you, sweet sirs, that he may not die?

MARY BEATON
Madam, for me I would not have him live;
Mine own heart's life was ended with my fame,
And my life's breath will shortly follow them;
So that I care not much; for you wot well
I have lost love and shame and fame and all
To no good end; nor while he had his life
Have I got good of him that was my love,
Save that for courtesy (which may God quit)
He kissed me once as one might kiss for love
Out of great pity for me; saving this,
He never did me grace in all his life.
And when you have slain him, madam, it may be
I shall get grace of him in some new way
In a new place, if God have care of us.

QUEEN
Bid you my brother to me presently.

[Exeunt **MARIES**.]

And yet the thing is pitiful; I would
There were some way. To send him overseas,
Out past the long firths to the cold keen sea
Where the sharp sound is that one hears up here—
Or hold him in strong prison till he died—
He would die shortly—or to set him free
And use him softly till his brains were healed—
There is no way. Now never while I live

Shall we twain love together any more
Nor sit at rhyme as we were used to do,
Nor each kiss other only with the eyes
A great way off ere hand or lip could reach;
There is no way.

[Enter **MURRAY**]

O, you are welcome, sir;
You know what need I have; but I praise heaven,
Having such need, I have such help of you.
I do believe no queen God ever made
Was better holpen than I look to be.
What, if two brethren love not heartily,
Who shall be good to either one of them?

MURRAY
Madam, I have great joy of your good will.

QUEEN
I pray you, brother, use no courtesies:
I have some fear you will not suffer me
When I shall speak. Fear is a fool, I think,
Yet hath he wit enow to fool my wits,
Being but a woman's. Do not answer me
Till you shall know; yet if you have a word
I shall be fain to heart it; but I think
There is no word to help me; no man's word:
There be two things yet that should do me good,
A speeding arm and a great heart. My lord,
I am soft-spirited as women are,
And ye wot well I have no harder heart:
Yea, with all my will I would not slay a thing,
But all should live right sweetly if I might;
So that man's blood-spilling lies hard on me.
I have a work yet for mine honor's sake,
A thing to do, God wot I know not how,
Nor how to crave it of you: nay, by heaven,
I will not shame myself to show it you:
I have not heart.

MURRAY
Why, if it may be done
With any honor, or with good men's excuse,
I shall well do it.

QUEEN
I would I wist that well.

Sir, do you love me?

MURRAY
Yea, you know I do.

QUEEN
In faith, you should well love me, for I love
The least man in your following for your sake
With a whole sister's heart.

MURRAY
Speak simply, madam;
I must obey you, being your bounden man.

QUEEN
Sir, so it is you know what things have been,
Even to the endangering of mine innocent name,
And by no fault, but by men's evil will;
If Chastelard have trial openly,
I am but shamed.

MURRAY
This were a wound indeed,
If your good name should lie upon his lip.

QUEEN
I will the judges put him not to plead,
For my fame's sake; he shall not answer them.

MURRAY
What, think you he will speak against your fame?

QUEEN
I know not; men might feign belief of him
For hate of me; it may be he will speak;
In brief, I will not have him held to proof.

MURRAY
Well, if this be, what good is to be done?

QUEEN
Is there no way but he must speak to them,
Being had to trial plainly?

MURRAY
I think, none.

QUEEN

Now mark, my lord; I swear he will not speak.

MURRAY
It were the best if you could make that sure.

QUEEN
There is one way. Look, sir, he shall not do it:
Shall not, or will not, either is one way;
I speak as I would have you understand.

MURRAY
Let me not guess at you; speak certainly.

QUEEN
You will not mind me: let him be removed;
Take means to get me surety; there be means.

MURRAY
So, in your mind, I have to slay the man?

QUEEN
Is there a mean for me to save the man?

MURRAY
Truly I see no mean except your love.

QUEEN
What love is that, my lord? what think you of,
Talking of love and of love's mean in me
And of your guesses and of slaying him?
Why, I say nought, have nought to say: God help me!
I bid you but take surety of the man,
Get him removed.

MURRAY
Come, come, be clear with me;
You bid me to despatch him privily.

QUEEN
God send me sufferance! I bid you, sir?
Nay, do not go; what matter if I did?
Nathless I never bade you; no, by God.
Be not so wroth; you are my brother born;
Why do you dwell upon me with such eyes?
For love of God you should not bear me hard.

MURRAY
What, are you made of flesh?

QUEEN
O, now I see
You had rather lose your wits to do me harm
Than keep sound wits to help me.

MURRAY
It is right strange;
The worst man living hath some fear, some love,
Holds somewhat dear a little for life's sake,
Keeps fast to some compassion; you have none;
You know of nothing that remembrance knows
To make you tender. I must slay the man?
Nay, I will do it.

QUEEN
Do, if you be not mad.
I am sorry for him; and he must needs die.
I would I were assured you hate me not:
I have no heart to slay him by my will.
I pray you think not bitterly of me.

MURRAY
Is it your pleasure such a thing were done?

QUEEN
Yea, by God's body is it, certainly.

MURRAY
Nay, for your love then, and for honor's sake,
This thing must be.

QUEEN
Yea, should I set you on?
Even for my love then, I beseech you, sir,
To seek him out, and lest he prate of me
To put your knife into him ere he come forth:
Meseems this were not such wild work to do.

MURRAY
I'll have him in the prison taken off.

QUEEN
I am bounden to you, even for my name's sake,
When that is done.

MURRAY
I pray you fear me not.

Farewell. I would such things were not to do,
Or not for me; yea, not for any man.

[Exit.]

QUEEN
Alas, what honor have I to give thanks?
I would he had denied me: I had held my peace
Thenceforth forever; but he wrung out the word,
Caught it before my lip, was fain of it—
It was his fault to put it in my mind,
Yea, and to feign a loathing of his fault.
Now is he about devising my love's death,
And nothing loth. Nay, since he must needs die,
Would he were dead and come alive again
And I might keep him safe. He doth live now
And I may do what love I will to him;
But by to-morrow he will be stark dead,
Stark slain and dead; and for no sort of love
Will he so much as kiss me half a kiss.
Were this to do I would not do it again.

[Re-enter **MURRAY**]

What, have you taken order? is it done?
It were impossible to do so soon.
Nay, answer me.

MURRAY
Madam, I will not do it.

QUEEN
How did you say? I pray, sir, speak again:
I know not what you said.

MURRAY
I say I will not;
I have thought thereof, and have made up my heart
To have no part in this: look you to it.

QUEEN
O, for God's sake! you will not have me shamed?

MURRAY
I will not dip my hand into your sin.

QUEEN
It were a good deed to deliver me;

I am but a woman, of one blood with you,
A feeble woman; put me not to shame;
I pray you of your pity do me right.
Yea, and no fleck of blood shall cleave to you
For a just deed.

MURRAY
I know not; I will none.

QUEEN
O, you will never let him speak to them
To put me in such shame? why, I should die
Out of pure shame and mine own burning blood;
Yea, my face feels the shame lay hold on it,
I am half burnt already in my thought;
Take pity of me. Think how shame slays a man;
How shall I live then? would you have me dead?
I pray you for our dead dear father's sake,
Let not men mock at me. Nay, if he speak,
I shall be sung in mine own towns. Have pity.
What, will you let men stone me in the ways?

MURRAY
Madam, I shall take pains the best I may
To save your honor, and what thing lieth in me
That will I do, but no close manslayings.
I will not have God's judgment gripe my throat
When I am dead, to hale me into hell
For a man's sake slain on this wise. Take heed.
See you to that.

[Exit.]

QUEEN
One of you maidens there
Bid my lord hither. Now by Mary's soul,
He shall not die and bring me into shame.
There's treason in you like a fever, hot,
My holy-natured brother, cheek and eye;
You look red through with it: sick, honor-sick,
Specked with the blain of treason, leper-like—
A scrupulous fair traitor with clean lips—
If one should sue to hell to do him good
He were as brotherly holpen as I am.
This man must live and say no harm of me;
I may reprieve and cast him forth; yea, so—
This were the best; or if he die midway—
Yea, anything, so that he die not here.

[To the **MARIES** within.]

Fetch hither Darnley. Nay, ye gape on me—
What, doth he sleep, or feeds, or plays at games?
Why, I would see him; I am weary for his sake;
Bid my lord in.—Nathless he will but chide;
Nay, fleer and laugh: what should one say to him?
There were some word if one could hit on it;
Some way to close with him: I wot not.—Sir,

[Enter **DARNLEY**]

Please it your love I have a suit to you.

DARNLEY
What sort of suit?

QUEEN
Nay, if you be not friends—
I have no suit towards mine enemies.

DARNLEY
Eh, do I look now like your enemy?

QUEEN
You have a way of peering under brow
I do not like. If you see anything
In me that irks you I will painfully
Labor to lose it: do but show me favor,
And as I am your faithful humble wife
This foolishness shall be removed in me.

DARNLEY
Why do you laugh and mock me with stretched hands?
Faith, I see no such thing.

QUEEN
That is well seen.
Come, I will take my heart between my lips,
Use it not hardly. Sir, my suit begins;
That you would please to make me that I am,
(In sooth I think I am) mistress and queen
Of mine own people.

DARNLEY
Why, this is no suit;
This is a simple matter, and your own.

QUEEN

It was, before God made you king of me.

DARNLEY

No king, by God's grace; were I such a king
I'd sell my kingdom for six roods of rye.

QUEEN

You are too sharp upon my words; I would
Have leave of you to free a man condemned.

DARNLEY

What man is that, sweet?

QUEEN

Such a mad poor man
As God desires us use not cruelly.

DARNLEY

Is there no name a man may call him by?

QUEEN

Nay, my fair master, what fair game is this?
Why, you do know him, it is Chastelard.

DARNLEY

Ay, is it soothly?

QUEEN

By my life, it is;
Sweet, as you tender me, so pardon him.

DARNLEY

As he doth tender you, so pardon me;
For if it were the mean to save my life
He should not live a day.

QUEEN

Nay, shall not he?

DARNLEY

Look what an evil wit old Fortune hath:
Why, I came here to get his time cut off.
This second fault is meat for lewd men's mouths;
You were best have him slain at once: 'tis hot.

QUEEN

Give me the warrant, and sit down, my lord.
Why, I will sign it; what, I understand
How this must be. Should not my name stand here?

DARNLEY
Yea, there, and here the seal.

QUEEN
Ay, so you say.
Shall I say too what I am thinking of?

DARNLEY
Do, if you will.

QUEEN
I do not like your suit.

DARNLEY
'Tis of no Frenchman fashion.

QUEEN
No, God wot;
'Tis nowise great men's fashion in French land
To clap a headsman's taberd on their backs.

DARNLEY
No, madam?

QUEEN
No; I never wist of that.
Is it a month gone I did call you lord?
I chose you by no straying stroke of sight,
But with my heart to love you heartily.
Did I wrong then? did mine eye draw my heart?
I know not; sir, it may be I did wrong:
And yet to love you; and would choose again,
Against to choose you.

DARNLEY
There, I love you too;
Take that for sooth, and let me take this hence.

QUEEN
O, do you think I hold you off with words?
Why, take it then; there is my handwriting,
And here the hand that you shall slay him with.
'Tis a fair hand, a maiden-colored one:
I doubt yet it has never slain a man.

You never fought yet save for game, I wis.
Nay, thank me not, but have it from my sight;
Go and make haste for fear he be got forth:
It may be such a man is dangerous;
Who knows what friends he hath? and by my faith
I doubt he hath seen some fighting, I do fear
He hath fought and shed men's blood; ye are wise men
That will not leave such dangerous things alive;
'T were well he died the sooner for your sakes.
Pray you make haste; it is not fit he live.

DARNLEY
What, will you let him die so easily?

QUEEN
Why, God have mercy! what way should one take
To please such people? there's some cunning way,
Something I miss, out of my simple soul.
What, must one say "Beseech you do no harm,"
Or "for my love, sweet cousins, be not hard,"
Or "let him live but till the vane come round"—
Will such things please you? well then, have your way;
Sir, I desire you, kneeling down with tears,
With sighs and tears, fair sir, require of you,
Considering of my love I bear this man,
Just for my love's sake let him not be hanged
Before the sundown; do thus much for me,
To have a queen's prayers follow after you.

DARNLEY
I know no need for you to gibe at me.

QUEEN
Alack, what heart then shall I have to jest?
There is no woman jests in such a wise—
For the shame's sake I pray you hang him not,
Seeing how I love him, save indeed in silk,
Sweet twisted silk of my sad handiwork.
Nay, and you will not do so much for me;
You vex your lip, biting the blood and all:
Were this so hard, and you compassionate?
I am in sore case then, and will weep indeed.

DARNLEY
What do you mean to cast such gibes at me?

QUEEN
Woe's me, and will you turn my tears to thorns?

Nay, set your eyes a little in my face;
See, do I weep? what will you make of me?
Will you not swear I love this prisoner?
Ye are wise, and ye will have it; yet for me
I wist not of it. We are but feeble fools,
And love may catch us when we lie asleep
And yet God knows we know not this a whit.
Come, look on me, swear you believe it not:
It may be I will take your word for that.

DARNLEY
Do you not love him? nay, but verily?

QUEEN
Now then, make answer to me verily,
Which of us twain is wiser? for my part
I will not swear I love not, if you will;
Ye be wise men and many men, my lords,
And ye will have me love him, ye will swear
That I do love him; who shall say ye lie?
Look on your paper; maybe I have wept:
Doubtless I love your hanged man in my heart.
What, is the writing smutched or gone awry?
Or blurred—ay, surely so much—with one tear,
One little sharp tear strayed on it by chance?
Come, come, the man is deadly dangerous;
Let him die presently.

DARNLEY
You do not love him;
Well, yet he need not die; it were right hard
To hang the fool because you love him not.

QUEEN
You have keen wits and thereto courtesy
To catch me with. No, let this man not die;
It were no such perpetual praise to you
To be his doomsman and in doglike wise
Bite his brief life in twain.

DARNLEY
Truly it were not.

QUEEN
Then for your honor and my love of you
(Oh, I do love you! but you know not, sweet,
You shall see how much), think you for their sake
He may go free?

DARNLEY
How, freely forth of us?
But yet he loves you, and being mad with love
Makes matter for base mouths to chew upon:
'T were best he live not yet.

QUEEN
Will you say that?

DARNLEY
Why should he live to breed you bad reports?
Let him die first.

QUEEN
Sweet, for your sake, not so.

DARNLEY
Fret not yourself to pity; let him die.

QUEEN
Come, let him live a little; it shall be
A grace to us.

DARNLEY
By God he dies at once.

QUEEN
Now, by God's mother, if I respite him,
Though you were all the race of you in one
And had more tongues than hairs to cry on me
He should not lose a hair.

DARNLEY
This is mere mercy—
But you thank God you love him not a whit?

QUEEN
It shall be what it please; and if I please
It shall be anything. Give me the warrant.

DARNLEY
Nay, for your sake and love of you, not I,
To make it dangerous.

QUEEN
O, God' pity, sir!
You are tender of me; will you serve me so,

Against mine own will, show me so much love,
Do me good service that I loath being done,
Out of pure pity?

DARNLEY
Nay, your word shall stand.

QUEEN
What makes you gape so beastlike after blood?
Were you not bred up on some hangman's hire
And dicted with fleshmeats at his hand
And fed into a fool? Give me that paper.

DARNLEY
Now for that word I will not.

QUEEN
Nay, sweet love,
For your own sake be just a little wise;
Come, I beseech you.

DARNLEY
Pluck not at my hands.

QUEEN
No, that I will not: I am brain-broken, mad;
Pity my madness for sweet marriage-sake
And my great love's; I love you to say this;
I would not have you cross me, out of love.
But for true love should I not chafe indeed?
And now I do not.

DARNLEY
Yea, and late you chid,
You chafed and jested and blew soft and hard—
No, for that "fool" you shall not fool me so.

QUEEN
You are no churl, sweet, will you see me weep?
Look, I weep now; be friends with my poor tears,
Think each of them beseeches you of love
And hath some tongue to cry on you for love
And speak soft things; for that which loves not you
Is none of mine, not though they grow of grief
And grief of you; be not too hard with them.
You would not of your own heart slay a man;
Nay, if you will, in God's name make me weep,
I will not hate you; but at heart, sweet lord,

Be not at heart my sweet heart's enemy.
If I had many mighty men to friend
I would not plead too lovingly with you
To have your love.

DARNLEY
Why, yet you have my love.

QUEEN
Alas, what shall mine enemies do to me
If he be used so hardly of my friends?
Come, sir, you hate me; yet for all your hate
You cannot have such heart.

DARNLEY
What sort of heart?
I have no heart to be used shamefully
If you mean that.

QUEEN
Would God I loved you not;
You are too hard to be used lovingly.

DARNLEY
You are moved too much for such a little love
As you bear me.

QUEEN
God knows you do me wrong;
God knows the heart, sweet, that I love you with.
Hark you, fair sir, I'd have all well with you;
Do you not fear at sick men's time of night
What end may come? are you so sure of heart?
Is not your spirit surprisable in sleep?
Have you no evil dreams? Nay, look you, love,
I will not be flung off you heart and hand,
I am no snake: but tell me for your love
Have you no fancies how these things will end
In the pit's mouth? how all life-deeds will look
At the grave's edge that lets men into hell?
For my part, who am weak and woman-eyed,
It turns my soul tears: I doubt this blood
Fallen on our faces when we twain are dead
Will scar and burn them: yea, for heaven is sweet,
And loves sweet deeds that smell not of split blood.
Let us not kill: God that made mercy first
Pities the pitiful for their deed's sake.

DARNLEY

Get you some painting; with a cheek like this
You'll find no faith in listeners.

QUEEN

How, fair lord?

DARNLEY

I say that looking with this face of yours
None shall believe you holy; what, you talk,
Take mercy in your mouth, eat holiness,
Put God under your tongue and feed on heaven,
With fear and faith and—faith, I know not what—
And look as though you stood and saw men slain
To make you game and laughter; nay, your eyes
Threaten as unto blood. What will you do
To make men take your sweet word? pitiful—
You are pitiful as he that's hired for death
And loves the slaying yet better than the hire.

QUEEN

You are wise that live to threat and tell me so;
Do you love life too much?

DARNLEY

O, now you are sweet,
Right tender now: you love not blood nor death,
You are too tender.

QUEEN

Yea, too weak, too soft:
Sweet, do not mock me, for my love's sake; see
How soft a thing I am. Will you be hard?
The heart you have, has it no sort of fear?

DARNLEY

Take off your hand and let me go my way
And do the deed, and when the doing is past
I will come home and teach you tender things
Out of my love till you forget my wrath.
I will be angry when I see good need,
And will grow gentle after, fear not that:
You shall get no wrong of my wrongdoing.
So I take leave.

QUEEN

Take what you will; take all;
You have taken half my heart away with words:

Take all I have, and take no leave; I have
No leave to give: yea, shortly shall lack leave,
I think, to live; but I crave none of you;
I would have none: yet for the love I have,
If I get ever a man to show it you,
I pray God put you some day in my hand
That you may take that too.

DARNLEY
Well, as he please;
God keep you in such love; and so farewell.

[Exit.]

QUEEN
So fare I as your lover, but not well.—
Ah sweet, if God be ever good to me
To put you in my hand! I am come to shame;
Let me think now, and let my wits not go;
God, for dear mercy, let me not forget
Why I should be so angry; the dull blood
Beats at my face and blinds me—I am chafted to death,
And I am shamed; I shall go mad and die.
Truly I think I did kneel down, did pray,
Yea, weep (who knows?) it may be—all for that.
Yea, if I wept not, this was blood brake forth
And burnt mine eyelids; I will have blood back,
And wash them cool in the hottest of his heart,
Or I will slay myself: I cannot tell:
I have given gold for brass, and lo the pay
Cleaves to my fingers: there's no way to mend—
Not while life stays: would God that it were gone!
The fool will feed upon my fame and laugh;
Till one seal up his tongue and lips with blood,
He carries half my honor and good name
Between his teeth. Lord God, mine head will fail!
When have I done thus since I was alive?
And these ill times will deal but ill with me—
My old love slain, and never a new to help,
And my wits gone, and my blithe use of life,
And all the grace was with me. Love—perchance
If I save love I shall well save myself.
I could find heart to bid him take such fellows
And kill them to my hand. I was the fool
To sue to these and shame myself: God knows
I was a queen born, I will hold their heads
Here in my hands for this. Which of you waits?

[Enter **MARY BEATON** and **MARY CARMICHAEL**]

No maiden of them?—what, no more than this?

MARY CARMICHAEL
Madam, the lady Seyton is gone forth;
She is ill at heart with watching.

QUEEN
Ay, at heart—
All girls must have such tender sides to the heart
They break for one night's watching, ache to death
For an hour's pity, for a half-hour's love—
Wear out before the watches, die by dawn,
And ride at noon to burial. God's my pity!
Where's Hamilton? doth she ail too? at heart,
I warrant her at heart.

MARY BEATON
I know not, madam.

QUEEN
What, sick or dead? I am well holpen of you:
Come hither to me. What pale blood you have—
Is it for fear you turn such cheeks to me?
Why, if I were so loving, by my hand,
I would have set my head upon the chance,
And loosed him though I died. What will you do?
Have you no way?

MARY BEATON
None but your mercy.

QUEEN
Ay?
Why then the thing is piteous. Think, for God's sake—
Is there no loving way to fetch him forth?
Nay, what a white thin-blooded thing is love,
To help no more than this doth! Were I in love,
I would unbar the ways to-night and then
Laugh death to death to-morrow, mock him dead;
I think you love well with one half your heart,
And let fear keep the other. Hark you now,
You said there was some friend durst break my bars—
Some Scotch name—faith, as if I wist of it!
Ye have such heavy wits to help one with—
Some man that had some mean to save him by—
Tush, I must be at pains for you!

MARY BEATON
Nay, madam,
It were no boot; he will not be let forth.

QUEEN
I say, the name. O, Robert Erskine—yea,
A fellow of some heart: what saith he?

MARY BEATON
Madam,
The thing was sound all through, yea, all went well,
But for all prayers that we could make to him
He would not fly: we cannot get him forth.

QUEEN
Great God! that men should have such wits as this!
I have a mind to let him die for that;
And yet I wot not. Said he, he loathed his life?

MARY BEATON
He says your grace given would scathe yourself,
And little grace for such a grace as that
Be with the little of his life he kept
To cast off some time more unworthily.

QUEEN
God help me! what should wise folk do with him?
These men be weaker-witted than mere fools
When they fall mad once; yet by Mary's soul
I am sorrier for him than for men right wise.
God wot a fool that were more wise than he
Would love me something worse than Chastelard,
Ay, and his own soul better. Do you think
(There's no such other sort of fool alive)
That he may live?

MARY BEATON
Yea, by God's mercy, madam,
To your great praise and honor from all men
If you should keep him living.

QUEEN
By God's light,
I have good will to do it. Are you sure,
If I would pack him with a pardon hence,
He would speak well of me—not hint and halt,
Smile and look back, sigh and say love runs out,

But times have been—with some loose laugh cut short,
Bit off at lip—eh?

MARY BEATON
No, by heaven he would not.

QUEEN
You know how quickly one may be belied—
Faith, you should know it—I never thought the worst,
One may touch love and come with clean hands off—
But you should know it. What, he will not fly—
Not though I wink myself asleep, turn blind—
Which that I will I say not?

MARY BEATON
Nay, not he;
We had good hope to bring him well aboard,
Let him slip safe down by the firths to sea,
Out under Leith by night-setting, and thence
Take ship for France and serve there out of sight
In the new wars.

QUEEN
Ay, in the new French wars—
You wist thereof too, madam, with good leave—
A goodly bait to catch mine honor with
And let me wake up with my name bit through.
I had been much bounden to you twain, methinks,
But for my knight's sake and his love's; by God,
He shall not die in God's despite nor mine.
Call in our chief lords; bid one see to it:
Ay, and make haste.

[Exeunt **MARY BEATON** and **MARY CARMICHAEL**]

Now shall I try their teeth:
I have done with fear; now nothing but pure love
And power and pity shall have part in me;
I will not throw them such a spirit in flesh
To make their prey on. Though he be mad indeed,
It is the goodliest madness ever smote
Upon man's heart. A kingly knight—in faith,
Meseems my face can yet make faith in men
And break their brains with beauty: for a word,
An eyelid's twitch, an eye's turn, tie them fast
And make their souls cleave to me. God be thanked,
This air has not yet curdled all the blood
That went to make me fair. An hour agone,

I thought I had been forgotten of men's love
More than dead women's faces are forgot
Of after lovers. All men are not of earth:
For all the frost of fools and this cold land
There be some yet catch fever of my face
And burning for mine eyes' sake. I did think
My time was gone when men would dance to death
As to a music, and lie laughing down
In the grave and take their funerals for their feasts,
To get one kiss of me. I have some strength yet,
Though I lack power on men that lack men's blood.
Yea, and God wot I will be merciful;
For all the foolish hardness round my heart
That tender women miss of to their praise,
They shall not say but I had grace to give
Even for love's sake. Why, let them take their way:
What ails it them though I be soft or hard?
Soft hearts would weep and weep and let men die
For very mercy and sweet-heartedness;
I that weep little for my pity's sake,
I have the grace to save men. Let fame go—
I care not much what shall become of fame,
So I save love and do mine own soul right;
I'll have my mercy help me to revenge
On all the crew of them. How will he look,
Having my pardon! I shall have sweet thanks
And love of good men for my mercy's love—
Yea, and be quit of these I hate to death,
With one good deed.

[Enter the **MARIES**.]

MARY BEATON
Madam, the lords are here.

QUEEN
Stand you about me, I will speak to them.
I would the whole world stood up in my face
And heard what I shall say. Bid them come in.

[Enter **MURRAY**, **RANDOLPH**, **MORTON**, **LINDSAY**, and other **LORDS**.]

Hear you, fair lords, I have a word to you;
There is one thing I would fain understand—
If I be queen or no; for by my life
Methinks I am growing unqueenly. No man speak?
Pray you take note, sweet lord ambassador,
I am no queen: I never was born queen;

Alack, that one should fool us in this wise!
Take up my crown, sir, I will none of it
Till it hath bells on as a fool's cap hath.
Nay, who will have it? no man take it up?
Was there none worthy to be shamed but I?
Here are enow good faces, good to crown;
Will you be king, fair brother? or you, my lord?
Give me a spinner's curch, a wisp of reed,
Any mean thing; but, God's love, no more gold,
And no more shame: let boys throw dice for it,
Or cast it to the grooms for tennis-play,
For I will none.

MURRAY
What would your highness have?

QUEEN
Yea, yea, I said I was no majesty;
I shall be shortly fallen out of grace.
What would I have? I would have leave to live;
Perchance I shall not shortly: nay, for me
That have no leave to respite other lives
To keep mine own life were small praise enow.

MURRAY
Your majesty hath power to respite men,
As we well wot; no man saith otherwise.

QUEEN
What, is this true? 't is a thing wonderful—
So great I cannot be well sure of it.
Strange that a queen should find such grace as this
At such lords' hands as ye be, such great lords:
I pray you let me get assured again,
Lest I take jest for truth and shame myself
And make you mirth: to make your mirth of me,
God wot it were small pains to you, my lords,
But much less honor. I may send reprieve—
With your sweet leaves I may?

MURRAY
Assuredly.

QUEEN
Lo, now, what grace is this I have of you!
I had a will to respite Chastelard,
And would not do it for very fear of you:
Look you, I wist not ye were merciful.

MORTON.
Madam—

QUEEN
My lord, you have a word to me?
Doth it displease you such a man should live?

MORTON.
'T were a mad mercy in your majesty
To lay no hand upon his second fault
And let him thrice offend you.

QUEEN
Ay, my lord?

MORTON.
It were well done to muffle lewd men's mouths
By casting of his head into their laps:
It were much best.

QUEEN
Yea, truly were it so?
But if I will not, yet I will not, sir,
For all the mouths in Scotland. Now, by heaven,
As I am pleased he shall not die but live,
So shall ye be. There is no man shall die,
Except it please me; and no man shall say,
Except it please me, if I do ill or well.
Which of you now will set his will to mine?
Not you, nor you I think, nor none of you,
Nor no man living that loves living well.
Let one stand forth and smite me with his hand,
Wring my crown off and cast it underfoot,
And he shall get my respite back of me,
And no man else: he shall bid live or die,
And no man else; and he shall be my lord,
And no man else. What, will not one be king?
Will not one here lay hold upon my state?
I am queen of you for all things come and gone.
Nay, my chief lady, and no meaner one,
The chiefest of my maidens, shall bear this
And give it to my prisoner for a grace;
Who shall deny me? who shall do me wrong?
Bear greeting to the lord of Chastelard,
And this withal for respite of his life,
For by my head he shall die no such way:
Nay, sweet, no words, but hence and back again.

[Exit **MARY BEATON**]

Farewell, dear lords; ye have shown grace to me,
And some time I will thank you as I may;
Till when think well of me and what is done.

ACT V - CHASTELARD

SCENE I.—Before Holyrood.

A crowd of people; among them **SOLDIERS**, **BURGESSES**, a **PREACHER**, &c.

1st CITIZEN
They are not out yet. Have you seen the man?
What manner of man?

2nd CITIZEN
Shall he be hanged or no?
There was a fellow hanged some three days gone
Wept the whole way: think you this man shall die
In better sort, now?

1st CITIZEN
Eh, these shawm-players
That walk before strange women and make songs!
How should they die well?

3rd CITIZEN
Is it sooth men say
Our dame was wont to kiss him on the face
In lewd folk's sight?

1st CITIZEN
Yea, saith one, all day long
He used to sit and jangle words in rhyme
To suit with shakes of faint adulterous sound
Some French lust in men's ears; she made songs too,
Soft things to feed sin's amorous mouth upon—
Delicate sounds for dancing at in hell.

4th CITIZEN
Is it priest Black that he shall have by him
When they do come?

3rd CITIZEN

Ah! by God's leave, not so;
If the knave show us his peeled onion's head
And that damned flagging jowl of his—

2nd CITIZEN
Nay, sirs,
Take heed of words; moreover, please it you,
This man hath no pope's part in him.

3rd CITIZEN
I say
That if priest whore's friend with the lewd thief's cheek
Show his foul blinking face to shame all ours,
It goes back fouler; well, one day hell's fire
Will burn him black indeed.

A WOMAN
What kind of man?
'T is yet great pity of him if he be
Goodly enow for this queen's paramour.
A French lord overseas? what doth he here,
With Scotch folk here?

1st CITIZEN
Fair mistress, I think well
He doth so at some times that I were fain
To do as well.

THE WOMAN
Nay, then he will not die.

1st CITIZEN
Why, see you, if one eat a piece of bread
Baked as it were a certain prophet's way,
Not upon coals, now—you shall apprehend—
If defiled bread be given a man to eat,
Being thrust into his mouth, why he shall eat,
And with good hap shall eat; but if now, say,
One steal this, bread and beastliness and all,
When scarcely for pure hunger flesh and bone
Cleave one to other—why, if he steal to eat,
Be it even the filthiest feeding—though the man
Be famine-flayed of flesh and skin, I say
He shall be hanged.

3rd CITIZEN
Nay, stolen said you, sir?
See, God bade eat abominable bread,

And freely was it eaten—for a sign
This, for a sign—and doubtless as did God,
So may the devil; bid one eat freely and live,
Not for a sign.

2nd CITIZEN
Will you think thus of her?
But wherefore should they get this fellow slain
If he be clear toward her?

3rd CITIZEN
Sir, one must see
The day comes when a woman sheds her sin
As a bird moults; and she being shifted so,
The old mate of her old feather pecks at her
To get the right bird back; then she being stronger
Picks out his eyes—eh?

2nd CITIZEN
Like enough to be;
But if it be—Is not one preaching there
With certain folk about him?

1st CITIZEN
Yea, the same
Who preached a month since from Ezekiel
Concerning these twain—this our queen that is
And her that was, and is not now so much
As queen over hell's worm.

3rd CITIZEN
Ay, said he not,
This was Aholah, the first one of these,
Called sisters only for a type—being twain,
Twain Maries, no whit Nazarine? the first
Bred out of Egypt like the water-worm
With sides in wet green places baked with slime
And festered flesh that steams against the sun;
A plague among all people, and a type
Set as a flake upon a leper's fell.

1st CITIZEN
Yea, said he, and unto her the men went in,
The men of Pharaoh's, beautiful with red
And with red gold, fair foreign-footed men,
The bountiful fair men, the courteous men,
The delicate men with delicate feet, that went
Curling their small beards Agag—fashion, yea

Pruning their mouths to nibble words behind
With pecking at God's skirts—small broken oaths
Fretted to shreds between most dainty lips,
And underbreath some praise of Ashtaroth
Sighed laughingly.

2nd CITIZEN
Was he not under guard
For the good word?

1st CITIZEN
Yea, but now forth again.—
And of the latter said he—there being two,
The first Aholah, which interpreted—

3rd CITIZEN
But, of this latter?

1st CITIZEN
Well, of her he said
How she made letters for Chaldean folk
And men that came forth of the wilderness
And all her sister's chosen men; yea, she
Kept not her lip from any sin of hers
But multiplied in whoredoms toward all these
That hate God mightily; for these, he saith,
These are the fair French people, and these her kin
Sought out of England with her love-letters
To bring them to her kiss of love; and thus
With a prayer made that God would break such love
Ended some while; then crying out for strong wrath
Spake with a great voice after: This is she,
Yea the lewd woman, yea the same woman
That gat bruised breasts in Egypt, when strange men
Swart from great suns, foot-burnt with angry soils
And strewn with sand of gaunt Chaldean miles,
Poured all their love upon her: she shall drink
The Lord's cup of derision that is filled
With drunkenness and sorrow, great of sides
And deep to drink in till the dreg drips out:
Yea, and herself with the twain shards thereof
Pluck off her breasts; so said he.

4th CITIZEN
See that stir—
Are not they come?

3rd CITIZEN

There wants an hour of them.
Draw near and let us hearken; he will speak
Surely some word of this.

2nd CITIZEN
What saith he now?

THE PREACHER
The mercy of a harlot is a sword;
And her mouth sharper than a flame of fire.

SCENE II.—In Prison.

CHASTELARD
So here my time shuts up; and the last light
Has made the last shade in the world for me.
The sunbeam that was narrow like a leaf
Has turned a hand, and the hand stretched to an arm,
And the arm has reached the dust on the floor, and made
A maze of motes with paddling fingers. Well,
I knew now that a man so sure to die
Could care so little; a bride-night's lustiness
Leaps in my veins as light fire under a wind:
As if I felt a kindling beyond death
Of some new joys far outside of me yet;
Sweet sound, sweet smell and touch of things far out
Sure to come soon. I wonder will death be
Even all it seems now? or the talk of hell
And wretched changes of the worn-out soul
Nailed to decaying flesh, shall that be true?
Or is this like the forethought of deep sleep
Felt by a tired man? Sleep were good enough—
Shall sleep be all? But I shall not forget
For any sleep this love bound upon me—
For any sleep or quiet ways of death.
Ah, in my weary dusty space of sight
Her face will float with heavy scents of hair
And fire of subtle amorous eyes, and lips
More hot than wine, full of sweet wicked words
Babbled against mine own lips, and long hands
Spread out, and pale bright throat and pale bright breasts,
Fit to make all men mad. I do believe
This fire shall never quite burn out to the ash
And leave no heat and flame upon my dust
For witness where a man's heart was burnt up.
For all Christ's work this Venus is not quelled,

But reddens at the mouth with blood of men,
Sucking between small teeth the sap o' the veins,
Dabbling with death her little tender lips—
A bitter beauty, poisonous-pearled mouth.
I am not fit to live but for love's sake,
So I were best die shortly. Ah, fair love,
Fair fearful Venus made of deadly foam,
I shall escape you somehow with my death—
Your splendid supple body and mouth on fire
And Paphian breath that bites the lips with heat.
I had best die.

[Enter **MARY BEATON**]

What, is my death's time come,
And you the friend to make death kind to me?
'T is sweetly done; for I was sick for this.

MARY BEATON
Nay, but see here; nay, for you shall not die:
She has reprieved you; look, her name to that,
A present respite; I was sure of her:
You are quite safe: here, take it in your hands:
I am faint with the end of pain. Read there.

CHASTELARD
Reprieve?
  Wherefore reprieve? Who has done this to me?

MARY BEATON
I never feared but God would have you live,
Or I knew well God must have punished me;
But I feared nothing, had no sort of fear.
What makes you stare upon the seal so hard?
Will you not read now?

CHASTELARD
A reprieve of life—
Reprieving me from living. Nay, by God,
I count one death a bitter thing enough.

MARY BEATON
See what she writes; you love; for love of you;
Out of her love; a word to save your life:
But I knew this too though you love me not:
She is your love; I knew that: yea, by heaven.

CHASTELARD

You knew I had to live and be reprieved:
Say I were bent to die now?

MARY BEATON
Do not die,
For her sweet love's sake; not for pity of me,
You would not bear with life for me one hour;
But for hers only.

CHASTELARD
Nay, I love you well,
I would not hurt you for more lives than one.
But for this fair-faced paper of reprieve,
We'll have no riddling to make death shift sides:
Look, here ends one of us.

[Tearing it.]

For her I love,
She will not anger heaven with slaying me;
For me, I am well quit of loving her;
For you, I pray you be well comforted,
Seeing in my life no man gat good by me
And by my death no hurt is any man's.

MARY BEATON
And I that loved you? nay, I loved you; nay,
Why should your like be pitied when they love?
Her hard heart is not yet so hard as yours,
Nor God's hard heart. I care not if you die.
These bitter madmen are not fit to live.
I will not have you touch me, speak to me,
Nor take farewell of you. See you die well,
Or death will play with shame for you, and win,
And laugh you out of life. I am right glad
I never am to see you any more,
For I should come to hate you easily;
I would not have you live.

[Exit.]

CHASTELARD
She has cause enow.
I would this wretched waiting had an end,
For I wax feebler than I was: God knows
I had a mind once to have saved this flesh
And made life one with shame. It marvels me
This girl that loves me should desire so much

To have me sleep with shame for bedfellow
A whole life's space; she would be glad to die
To escape such life. It may be too her love
Is but an amorous quarrel with herself,
Not love of me but her own wilful soul;
Then she will live and be more glad of this
Than girls of their own will and their heart's love
Before love mars them: so God go with her!
For mine own love—I wonder will she come
Sad at her mouth a little, with drawn cheeks
And eyelids wrinkled up? or hot and quick
To lean her head on mine and leave her lips
Deep in my neck? For surely she must come;
And I should fare the better to be sure
What she will do. But as it please my sweet;
For some sweet thing she must do if she come,
Seeing how I have to die. Now three years since
This had not seemed so good an end for me;
But in some wise all things wear round betimes
And wind up well. Yet doubtless she might take
A will to come my way and hold my hands
And kiss me some three kisses, throat, mouth, eyes,
And say some soft three words to soften death:
I do not see how this should break her ease.
Nay, she will come to get her warrant back:
By this no doubt she is sorely penitent,
Her fit of angry mercy well blown out
And her wits cool again. She must have chafed
A great while through for anger to become
So like pure pity; they must have fretted her
Night mad for anger: or it may be mistrust,
She is so false; yea, to my death I think
She will not trust me; alas the hard sweet heart!
As if my lips could hurt her any way
But by too keenly kissing of her own.
Ah false poor sweet fair lips that keep no faith,
They shall not catch mine false or dangerous;
They must needs kiss me one good time, albeit
They love me not at all. Lo, here she comes,
For the blood leaps and catches at my face;
There go her feet and tread upon my heart;
Now shall I see what way I am to die.

[Enter the **QUEEN**]

QUEEN
What, is one here? Speak to me for God's sake:
Where are you lain?

CHASTELARD
Here, madam, at your hand.

QUEEN
Sweet lord, what sore pain have I had for you
And been most patient!—Nay, you are not bound.
If you be gentle to me, take my hand.
Do you not hold me the worst heart in the world?
Nay, you must needs; but say not yet you do.
I am worn so weak I know not how I live:
Reach me your hand.

CHASTELARD
Take comfort and good heart;
All will find end; this is some grief to you,
But you shall overlive it. Come, fair love;
Be of fair cheer: I say you have done no wrong.

QUEEN
I will not be of cheer: I have done a thing
That will turn fire and burn me. Tell me not;
If you will do me comfort, whet your sword.
But if you hate me, tell me of soft things,
For I hate these, and bitterly. Look up;
Am I not mortal to be gazed upon?

CHASTELARD
Yea, mortal, and not hateful.

QUEEN
O lost heart!
Give me some mean to die by.

CHASTELARD
Sweet, enough.
You have made no fault; life is not worth a world
That you should weep to take it: would mine were,
And I might give you a world-worthier gift
Than one poor head that love has made a spoil;
Take it for jest, and weep not: let me go,
And think I died of chance or malady.
Nay, I die well; one dies not best abed.

QUEEN,
My warrant to reprieve you—that you saw?
That came between your hands?

CHASTELARD
Yea, not long since.
It seems you have no will to let me die.

QUEEN
Alas, you know I wrote it with my heart,
Out of pure love; and since you were in bonds
I have had such grief for love's sake and my heart's—
Yea, by my life I have—I could not choose
But give love way a little. Take my hand;
You know it would have pricked my heart's blood out
To write reprieve with.

CHASTELARD
Sweet, your hands are kind;
Lay them about my neck, upon my face,
And tell me not of writing.

QUEEN
Nay, by heaven,
I would have given you mine own blood to drink
If that could heal you of your soul-sickness.
Yea, they know that, they curse me for your sake,
Rail at my love—would God their heads were lopped
And we twain left together this side death!
But look you, sweet, if this my warrant hold
You are but dead and shamed; for you must die,
And they will slay you shamefully by force
Even in my sight.

CHASTELARD
Faith, I think so they will.

QUEEN
Nay, they would slay me too, cast stones at me,
Drag me alive—they have eaten poisonous words,
They are mad and have no shame.

CHASTELARD
Ay, like enough.

QUEEN
Would God my heart were greater; but God wot
I have no heart to bear with fear and die.
Yea, and I cannot help you: or I know
I should be nobler, bear a better heart:
But as this stands—I pray you for good love,
As you hold honor a costlier thing than life—

CHASTELARD
Well?

QUEEN
Nay, I would not be denied for shame;
In brief, I pray you give me that again.

CHASTELARD
What, my reprieve?

QUEEN
Even so; deny me not,
For your sake mainly: yea, by God you know
How fain I were to die in your death's stead.
For your name's sake. This were no need to swear.
Lest we be mocked to death with a reprieve,
And so both die, being shamed. What, shall I swear?
What, if I kiss you? must I pluck it out?
You do not love me: no, nor honor. Come
I know you have it about you: give it me.

CHASTELARD
I cannot yield you such a thing again;
Not as I had it.

QUEEN
A coward? what shift now?
Do such men make such cravens?

CHASTELARD
Chide me not:
Pity me that I cannot help my heart.

QUEEN
Heaven mend mine eyes that took you for a man!
What, is it sewn into your flesh? take heed—
Nay, but for shame—what have you done with it?

CHASTELARD
Why, there it lies, torn up.

QUEEN
God help me, sir!
Have you done this?

CHASTELARD
Yea, sweet; what should I do?

Did I not know you to the bone, my sweet?
God speed you well! you have a goodly lord.

QUEEN
My love, sweet love, you are more fair than he,
Yea, fairer many times: I love you much,
Sir, know you that.

CHASTELARD
I think I know that well.
Sit here a little till I feel you through
In all my breath and blood for some sweet while.
O gracious body that mine arms have had,
And hair my face has felt on it! grave eyes
And low thick lids that keep since years agone
In the blue sweet of each particular vein
Some special print of me! I am right glad
That I must never feel a bitterer thing
Than your soft curled-up shoulder and amorous arms
From this time forth; nothing can hap to me
Less good than this for all my whole life through.
I would not have some new pain after this
Come spoil the savor. O, your round bird's throat,
More soft than sleep or singing; your calm cheeks,
Turned bright, turned wan with kisses hard and hot;
The beautiful color of your deep curved hands,
Made of a red rose that had changed to white;
That mouth mine own holds half the sweetness of,
Yea, my heart holds the sweetness of it, whence
My life began in me; mine that ends here
Because you have no mercy, nay you know
You never could have mercy. My fair love,
Kiss me again, God loves you not the less;
Why should one woman have all goodly things?
You have all beauty; let mean women's lips
Be pitiful, and speak truth: they will not be
Such perfect things as yours. Be not ashamed
That hands not made like these that snare men's souls
Should do men good, give alms, relieve men's pain;
You have the better, being more fair than they,
They are half foul, being rather good than fair;
You are quite fair: to be quite fair is best.
Why, two nights hence I dreamed that I could see
In through your bosom under the left flower,
And there was a round hollow, and at heart
A little red snake sitting, without spot,
That bit—like this, and sucked up sweet—like this,
And curled its lithe light body right and left,

And quivered like a woman in act to love.
Then there was some low fluttered talk i' the lips,
Faint sound of soft fierce words caressing them—
Like a fair woman's when her love gets way.
Ah, your old kiss—I know the ways of it:
Let the lips cling a little. Take them off,
And speak some word or I go mad with love.

QUEEN
Will you not have my chaplain come to you?

CHASTELARD
Some better thing of yours—some handkerchief,
Some fringe of scarf to make confession to—
You had some book about you that fell out—

QUEEN
A little written book of Ronsard's rhymes,
His gift, I wear in there for love of him—
See, here between our feet.

CHASTELARD
Ay, my old lord's—
The sweet chief poet, my dear friend long since?
Give me the book. Lo you, this verse of his:
With coming lilies in late April came
Her body, fashioned whiter for their shame;
And roses, touched with blood since Adon bled,
From her fair color filled their lips with red:
A goodly praise: I could not praise you so.
I read that while your marriage-feast went on.
Leave me this book, I pray you: I would read
The hymn of death here over ere I die;
I shall know soon how much he knew of death
When that was written. One thing I know now,
I shall not die with half a heart at least,
Nor shift my face, nor weep my fault alive,
Nor swear if I might live and do new deeds
I would do better. Let me keep the book.

QUEEN
Yea, keep it: as would God you had kept your life
Out of mine eyes and hands. I am wrong to the heart:
This hour feels dry and bitter in my mouth,
As if its sorrow were my body's food
More than my soul's. There are bad thoughts in me—
Most bitter fancies biting me like birds
That tear each other. Suppose you need not die?

CHASTELARD

You know I cannot live for two hours more.
Our fate was made thus ere our days were made:
Will you fight fortune for so small a grief?
But for one thing I were full fain of death.

QUEEN

What thing is that?

CHASTELARD

No need to name the thing.
Why, what can death do with me fit to fear?
For if I sleep I shall not weep awake;
Or if their saying be true of things to come,
Though hell be sharp, in the worst ache of it
I shall be eased so God will give me back
Sometimes one golden gracious sight of you—
The aureole woven flowerlike through your hair,
And in your lips the little laugh as red
As when it came upon a kiss and ceased,
Touching my mouth.

QUEEN

As I do now, this way,
With my heart after: would I could shed tears,
Tears should not fail when the heart shudders so.
But your bad thought?

CHASTELARD

Well, such a thought as this:
It may be, long time after I am dead,
For all you are, you may see bitter days;
God may forget you or be wroth with you:
Then shall you lack a little help of me,
And I shall feel your sorrow touching you,
A happy sorrow, though I may not touch:
I that would fain be turned to flesh again,
Fain get back life to give up life for you,
To shed my blood for help, that long ago
You shed and were not holpen: and your heart
Will ache for help and comfort, yea for love,
And find less love than mine—for I do think
You never will be loved thus in your life.

QUEEN

It may be man will never love me more;
For I am sure I shall not love man twice.

CHASTELARD

I know not: men must love you in life's spite;
For you will always kill them; man by man
Your lips will bite them dead; yea, though you would,
You shall not spare one; all will die of you;
I cannot tell what love shall do with these,
But I for all my love shall have no might
To help you more, mine arms and hands no power
To fasten on you more. This cleaves my heart,
That they shall never touch your body more.
But for your grief—you will not have to grieve;
For being in such poor eyes so beautiful
It must needs be as God is more than I
So much more love he hath of you than mine;
Yea, God shall not be bitter with my love,
Seeing she is so sweet.

QUEEN

Ah my sweet fool,
Think you when God will ruin me for sin
My face of color shall prevail so much
With him, so soften the toothed iron's edge
To save my throat a scar? nay, I am sure
I shall die somehow sadly.

CHASTELARD

This is pure grief;
The shadow of your pity for my death,
Mere foolishness of pity: all sweet moods
Throw out such little shadows of themselves,
Leave such light fears behind. You, die like me?
Stretch your throat out that I may kiss all round
Where mine shall be cut through: suppose my mouth
The axe-edge to bite so sweet a throat in twain
With bitter iron, should not it turn soft
As lip is soft to lip?

QUEEN

I am quite sure
I shall die sadly some day, Chastelard;
I am quite certain.

CHASTELARD

Do not think such things;
Lest all my next world's memories of you be
As heavy as this thought.

QUEEN
I will not grieve you;
Forgive me that my thoughts were sick with grief.
What can I do to give you ease at heart?
Shall I kiss now? I pray you have no fear
But that I love you.

CHASTELARD
Turn your face to me;
I do not grudge your face this death of mine;
It is too fair—by God, you are too fair.
What noise is that?

QUEEN
Can the hour be through so soon?
I bade them give me but a little hour.
Ah! I do love you! such brief space for love!
I am yours all through, do all your will with me;
What if we lay and let them take us fast,
Lips grasping lips? I dare do anything.

CHASTELARD
Show better cheer: let no man see you mazed;
Make haste and kiss me; cover up your throat
Lest one see tumbled lace and prate of it.

[Enter the Guard: **MURRAY**, **DARNLEY**, **MARY HAMILTON**, **MARY BEATON**, and **OTHERS** with them.]

DARNLEY
Sirs, do your charge; let him not have much time.

MARY HAMILTON
Peace, lest you chafe the queen: look, her brows bend.

CHASTELARD
Lords, and all you come hither for my sake,
If while my life was with me like a friend
That I must now forget the friendship of,
I have done a wrong to any man of you,
As it may be by fault of mine I have;
Of such an one I crave for courtesy
He will now cast it from his mind and heed
Like a dead thing; considering my dead fault
Worth no remembrance further than my death.
This for his gentle honor and goodwill
I do beseech him, doubting not to find
Such kindliness if he be nobly made
And of his birth a courteous race of man.

You, my Lord James, if you have aught toward me—
Or you, Lord Darnley—I dare fear no jot,
Whate'er this be wherein you were aggrieved,
But you will pardon all for gentleness.

DARNLEY
For my part—yea, well, if the thing stand thus,
As you must die—one would not bear folk hard—
And if the rest shall hold it honorable,
Why, I do pardon you.

MURRAY
Sir, in all things
We find no cause to speak of you but well:
For all I see, save this your deadly fault,
I hold you for a noble perfect man.

CHASTELARD
I thank you, fair lord, for your nobleness.
You likewise, for the courtesy you have
I give you thanks, sir; and to all these lords
That have not heart to load me at my death.
Last, I beseech of the best queen of men
And royallest fair lady in the world
To pardon me my grievous mortal sin
Done in such great offence of her: for, sirs,
If ever since I came between her eyes
She hath beheld me other than I am
Or shown her honor other than it is,
Or, save in royal faultless courtesies,
Used me with favor; if by speech or face,
By salutation or by tender eyes,
She hath made a way for my desire to live,
Given ear to me or boldness to my breath;
I pray God cast me forth before day cease
Even to the heaviest place there is in hell.
Yea, if she be not stainless toward all men,
I pray this axe that I shall die upon
May cut me off body and soul from heaven.
Now for my soul's sake I dare pray to you;
Forgive me, madam.

QUEEN
Yea, I do, fair sir:
With all my heart in all I pardon you.

CHASTELARD
God thank you for great mercies. Lords, set hence;

I am right loth to hold your patience here;
I must not hold much longer any man's.
Bring me my way and bid me fare well forth.

[As they pass out the **QUEEN** stays **MARY BEATON**]

QUEEN
Hark hither, sweet. Get back to Holyrood
And take Carmichael with you: go both up
In some chief window whence the squares lie clear—
Seem not to know what I shall do—mark that—
And watch how things fare under. Have good cheer;
You do not think now I can let him die?
Nay, this were shameful madness if you did,
And I should hate you.

MARY BEATON
Pray you love me, madam,
And swear you love me and will let me live,
That I may die the quicker.

QUEEN
Nay, sweet, see,
Nay, you shall see, this must not seem devised;
I will take any man with me, and go;
Yea, for pure hate of them that hate him: yea,
Lay hold upon the headsman and bid strike
Here on my neck; if they will have him die,
Why, I will die too: queens have died this way
For less things than his love is. Nay, I know
They want no blood; I will bring swords to boot
For dear love's rescue though half earth were slain;
What should men do with blood? Stand fast at watch;
For I will be his ransom if I die.

[Exeunt.]

SCENE III.—The Upper Chamber in Holyrood.

MARY BEATON seated; **MARY CARMICHAEL** at a window.

MARY BEATON
Do you see nothing?

MARY CARMICHAEL
Nay, but swarms of men

And talking women gathered in small space,
Flapping their gowns and gaping with fools' eyes:
And a thin ring round one that seems to speak,
Holding his hands out eagerly; no more.

MARY BEATON
Why, I hear more, I hear men shout The Queen.

MARY CARMICHAEL
Nay, no cries yet.

MARY BEATON
Ah, they will cry out soon
When she comes forth; they should cry out on her;
I hear their crying in my heart. Nay, sweet,
Do not you hate her? all men, if God please,
Shall hate her one day; yea, one day no doubt
I shall worse hate her.

MARY CARMICHAEL
Pray you, be at peace;
You hurt yourself: she will be merciful;
What, could you see a true man slain for you?
I think I could not; it is not like our hearts
To have such hard sides to them.

MARY BEATON
O, not you,
And I could nowise; there's some blood in her
That does not run to mercy as ours doth:
That fair face and the cursed heart in her
Made keener than a knife for manslaying
Can bear strange things.

MARY CARMICHAEL
Peace, for the people come.
Ah—Murray, hooded over half his face
With plucked-down hat, few folk about him, eyes
Like a man angered; Darnley after him,
Holding our Hamilton above her wrist,
His mouth put near her hair to whisper with—
And she laughs softly, looking at her feet.

MARY BEATON
She will not live long; God hath given her
Few days and evil, full of hate and love,
I see well now.

MARY CARMICHAEL

Hark, there's their cry—The Queen!
Fair life and long, and good days to the Queen!

MARY BEATON

Yea, but God knows. I feel such patience here
As I were sure in a brief while to die.

MARY CARMICHAEL

She bends and laughs a little, graciously,
And turns half, talking to I know not whom—
A big man with great shoulders; ah, the face,
You get his face now—wide and duskish, yea
The youth burnt out of it. A goodly man,
Thewed mightily and sunburnt to the bone;
Doubtless he was away in banishment,
Or kept some march far off.

MARY BEATON

Still you see nothing?

MARY CARMICHAEL

Yea, now they bring him forth with a great noise,
The folk all shouting and men thrust about
Each way from him.

MARY BEATON

Ah, Lord God, bear with me,
Help me to bear a little with my love
For thine own love, or give me some quick death.
Do not come down; I shall get strength again,
Only my breath fails. Looks he sad or blithe?
Not sad I doubt yet.

MARY CARMICHAEL

Nay, not sad a whit,
But like a man who losing gold or lands
Should lose a heavy sorrow; his face set,
The eyes not curious to the right or left,
And reading in a book, his hands unbound,
With short fleet smiles. The whole place catches breath,
Looking at him; she seems at point to speak:
Now she lies back, and laughs, with her brows drawn
And her lips drawn too. Now they read his crime—
I see the laughter tightening her chin:
Why do you bend your body and draw breath?
They will not slay him in her sight; I am sure
She will not have him slain.

MARY BEATON
Forth, and fear not:
I was just praying to myself—one word,
A prayer I have to say for her to God
If he will mind it.

MARY CARMICHAEL
Now he looks her side;
Something he says, if one could hear thus far:
She leans out, lengthening her throat to hear
And her eyes shining.

MARY BEATON
Ah, I had no hope:
Yea thou God knowest that I had no hope.
Let it end quickly.

MARY CARMICHAEL
Now his eyes are wide
And his smile great; and like another smile
The blood fills all his face. Her cheek and neck
Work fast and hard; she must have pardoned him,
He looks so merrily. Now he comes forth
Out of that ring of people and kneels down;
Ah, how the helve and edge of the great axe
Turn in the sunlight as the man shifts hands—
It must be for a show: because she sits
And hardly moves her head this way—I see
Her chin and lifted lips. Now she stands up,
Puts out her hand, and they fall muttering;
Ah!

MARY BEATON
Is it done now?

MARY CARMICHAEL
For God's love, stay there;
Do not look out. Nay, he is dead by this;
But gather up yourself from off the floor;
Will she die too? I shut mine eyes and heard—
Sweet, do not beat your face upon the ground.
Nay, he is dead and slain.

MARY BEATON
What, slain indeed?
I knew he would be slain. Ay, through the neck:
I knew one must be smitten through the neck

To die so quick: if one were stabbed to the heart,
He would die slower.

MARY CARMICHAEL
Will you behold him dead?

MARY BEATON
Yea: must a dead man not be looked upon
That living one was fain of? give me way.
Lo you, what sort of hair this fellow had;
The doomsman gathers it into his hand
To grasp the head by for all men to see;
I never did that.

MARY CARMICHAEL
For God's love, let me go.

MARY BEATON
I think sometimes she must have held it so,
Holding his head back, see you, by the hair
To kiss his face, still lying in his arms.
Ay, go and weep: it must be pitiful
If one could see it. What is this they say?
So perish the Queen's traitors! Yea, but so
Perish the Queen! God, do thus much to her
For his sake only: yea, for pity's sake
Do thus much with her.

MARY CARMICHAEL
Prithee come in with me:
Nay, come at once.

MARY BEATON
If I should meet with her
And spit upon her at her coming in—
But if I live then shall I see one day
When God will smite her lying harlot's mouth—
Surely I shall. Come, I will go with you;
We will sit down together face to face
Now, and keep silence; for this life is hard,
And the end of it is quietness at last.
Come, let us go: here is no word to say.

AN USHER
Make way there for the lord of Bothwell; room—
Place for my lord of Bothwell next the queen.

Algernon Charles Swinburne was born at 7 Chester Street, Grosvenor Place, in London, on April 5th, 1837. He was the eldest of six children born to Captain Charles Henry Swinburne and Lady Jane Henrietta, daughter of the 3rd Earl of Ashburnham, a wealthy Northumbrian family.

Swinburne spent his early years at East Dene in Bonchurch, on the Isle of Wight. As a child, Swinburne was nervous and frail, but also imbued with a nervous energy and fearlessness almost to the point of recklessness.

He was schooled at Eton College from 1849 to 1853.   It was here that he first began to write poetry. He excelled at languages and whilst still at Eton won first prizes in both French and Italian.

From Eton he moved to Oxford where he attended at Balliol College from 1856.   Here he met friends to whom he became closely attached, among them Dante Gabriel Rossetti, William Morris and Edward Burne-Jones, who in 1857, were painting their Arthurian murals on the walls of the Oxford Union.   At Oxford Swinburne was mentored by Benjamin Jowett, the master of Balliol College, who recognised his poetic talent and, intervening on his behalf, tried to keep him from being expelled when he celebrated the Italian patriot Orsini, and his failed attempt on the life of Napoleon III in 1858. Swinburne had to leave the Universcity for a few months due to this but returned in May, 1860 but never received a degree.

Summers were usually spent at Capheaton Hall in Northumberland, the house of his grandfather, Sir John Swinburne, 6th Baronet, who had a famous library and was himself President of the Literary and Philosophical Society in Newcastle upon Tyne.

Swinburne proudly considered himself a native of Northumberland and this is reflected in poems such as the intensely patriotic 'Northumberland' and 'Grace Darling'. He enjoyed riding across the moors and was, it was said, a daring horseman, as he moved 'through honeyed leagues of the northland border', as he remembered the Scottish border in his Recollections.

In the period from 1857 to 1860, Swinburne was one of a number of Pre-Raphaelite's who visited and became part of Lady Pauline Trevelyan's intellectual circle at Wallington Hall, a few miles west of Morpeth in Northumberland.

After leaving college, he moved to London and began his career in earnest as well as becoming a constant visitor to the Rossetti's house.   To Rossetti Swinburne was his 'little Northumbrian friend', an affectionate reference to Swinburne's small stature—a mere five foot four. Whatever Swinburne lacked in height he made up for in poetic talent.   However, with the burden of such great talent came the unveiling of a dark side that was to cause him pain and would, at times, threaten his very existence with all manner of self-inflicted pains through drink, drugs and sado-machoism.

In 1860 Swinburne published two verse dramas; The Queen Mother and Rosamond but it would not be until 1865 that Swinburne would achieve literary success with Atalanta in Calydon.

In 1861, Swinburne visited Menton on the French Riviera to recover from the effects of yet another period of excess use of alcohol, staying at the Villa Laurenti. From Menton, Swinburne then travelled on to Italy, where he journeyed widely.

After Elizabeth Rossetti's death from suicide in 1862, he and Rossetti moved to Tudor House at 16 Cheyne Walk in Chelsea. The stories that survive from his year with Rossetti are typical Swinburne.   In one, Rossetti once had to tell him to keep down the noise — he and a boyfriend had been sliding naked down the bannisters and disturbing Rossetti's painting. He took a sardonic delight in what the critic and biographer, Cecil Lang, calls "Algernonic exaggeration": When people began to talk scathingly about his homosexuality and other sexual proclivities, he circulated a story that he had engaged in pederasty and bestiality with a monkey — and then eaten it. How many of the stories were true and how many invented is unclear. Oscar Wilde called him "a braggart in matters of vice, who had done everything he could to convince his fellow citizens of his homosexuality and bestiality without being in the slightest degree a homosexual or a bestialiser."

In December 1862, Swinburne accompanied Scott and his guests on a trip to Tynemouth. Scott writes in his memoirs that, as they walked by the sea, Swinburne declaimed the as yet unpublished 'Hymn to Proserpine' and 'Laus Veneris' in his lilting intonation, while the waves 'were running the whole length of the long level sands towards Cullercoats and sounding like far-off acclamations'.

Swinburne possessed a curious combination of frail health and strength. He was small and slightly built, but an excellent swimmer and the first to climb Culver Cliff on the Isle of Wight. He had an extremely excitable disposition: people who met him described him as a "demoniac boy" who would go skipping about the room declaiming poetry at the top of his voice. In this as in many things, moderation was not the standard for him.   Excess was.   Once or twice he had fits, thought to be epileptic, in public; but he made this condition much worse by drinking past excess to unconsciousness. More than once he was delivered to the door in the small of the night, dead drunk. Throughout the 1860s and '70s he rode an alcoholic cycle of dissolution, collapse, drying out at home in the country, then returning to London where he would begin the cycle all over again.

His mania for masochism, particularly flagellation, most probably started in early childhood at Eton and was encouraged by his later friendships with Richard Monckton Milnes (one of Tennyson's fellow Apostles), who introduced him to the works of the Marquis de Sade, and Richard Burton, the Victorian explorer and adventurer. Swinburne was an alcoholic and algolagniac (a desire for sexual gratification through inflicting pain on oneself or others; sadomasochism). He found life difficult, unfulfilling but still his poetic talents pushed to the fore.

Although Swinburne continued to publish some works in periodicals in 1865 he was granted recognition by both public and critics with Atalanta in Calydon written in the style of a classical Greek tragedy.

There followed "Laus Veneris" and Poems and Ballads (1866), with their sexually charged passages, absolutely decadent for polite Victorian society, which were attacked all the more violently as a result. The poems written in homage of Sappho of Lesbos such as "Anactoria" and "Sapphics" were especially savaged. The volume also contained poems such as "The Leper," "Laus Veneris," and "St Dorothy" which evoke both Swinburne's and a general Victorian fascination with the Middle Ages, and are explicitly mediaeval in style, tone and construction. With its publication came instant notoriety. He was now identified with indecent and decadent themes and the precept of art for art's sake.

Swinburne's meeting in 1867 with his long-time hero Mazzini, the Italian patriot living in England in exile, was the beginning of a poetical journey that now became more serious and more engaged with serious thought, initially leading to the political poems in the volume Songs Before Sunrise.

Also in 1867 he was introduced to Adah Isaacs Menken, the American actress, poet and circus rider, whose main fame seemed to be riding naked on a horse (in fact she wore tight nude coloured clothing) for her performance in the melodrama Mazeppa (itself based on a poem by Lord Byron). Although they had a short affair Adah's quote implies that Swinburne was not ready for a relationship that did not involve some self-sabotage; "I can't make him understand that biting's no use."

In 1879, with Swinburne nearly dead from alcoholism and dissolution, his legal advisor Theodore Watts-Dunton took him in, and was gradually successful in getting him to adapt to a healthier lifestyle. Swinburne lived the rest of his life at Watts-Dunton's house. He saw less and less of his old bohemian friends, who thought him a prisoner at The Pines, but his growing deafness also accounts for some of his decreased sociability. By now Swinburne was 42, and was moving from a young man of rebelliousness to a figure of social respectability. It was said of Watts-Dunton that he saved the man and killed the poet.

It is clear that Swinburne had an addictive personality, and clearly incapable of moderation in his pursuit of any chosen vices. This, of course, would both nourish and perhaps sabotage his poetic career. His poetry follows the somewhat clichéd pattern of early flourish and later decline; indeed some of the fresher pieces in the second and third series of Poems and Ballads (published in 1878 and 1889) were actually written during his days at Oxford. Nevertheless, his last collection, A Channel Passage, has some beautiful poems, including "The Lake of Gaube."

He is best remembered as the supreme technician in metre, with a versatility which exceeds even Tennyson's, but which lacks a corresponding emotional range. His obsessions are not widely enough shared; and if he cannot shock us by the strangeness of his desires nor the shrillness of his anti-theistical exclamations, often what remains is not enough to fully engage with the audience.

Swinburne is considered a poet of the decadent school, although he perhaps professed to more vice than he actually indulged in to advertise his deviance. Common gossip of the time reported that he also had a deep crush on the explorer Sir Richard Francis Burton, despite the fact that Swinburne himself abhorred travel. Fact and fiction are easily absorbed by the other so are difficult to untangle even now.

Many critics consider his mastery of vocabulary, rhyme and metre impressive, although he has also been criticised for his florid style and word choices that only fit the rhyme scheme rather than contributing to the meaning of the piece. A. E. Housman, although a critic, had great praise for his rhyming ability: to Swinburne the sonnet was child's play: the task of providing four rhymes was not hard enough, and he wrote long poems in which each stanza required eight or ten rhymes, and wrote them so that he never seemed to be saying anything for the rhyme's sake.

Throughout his career Swinburne published literary criticism of great worth. His deep knowledge of world literatures contributed to a critical style rich in quotation, allusion, and comparison. He is particularly noted for discerning studies of Elizabethan dramatists and of many English and French poets and novelists. As well he was a noted essayist and wrote two novels.

Swinburne was nominated for the Nobel Prize in Literature every year from 1903 to 1907 and then again in 1909.

H.P. Lovecraft, the master of the dark side and a decent poet himself, considered Swinburne "the only real poet in either England or America after the death of Mr. Edgar Allan Poe."

Swinburne was also responsible for devising a poetic form called the roundel, a variation of the French Rondeau form.   In 1883 he published A Century of Roundels with several of the roundels dedicated to Dante's sister, the poet Christina Georgina Rossetti. Swinburne wrote to Edward Burne-Jones in 1883: "I have got a tiny new book of songs or songlets, in one form and all manner of metres ... just coming out, of which Miss Rossetti has accepted the dedication. I hope you and Georgie [his wife Georgiana] will find something to like among a hundred poems of nine lines each, twenty-four of which are about babies or small children".

Opinions of the Roundel poems move between those who find them captivating and brilliant, to others who find them merely clever and contrived. One of them, A Baby's Death, was set to music by the English composer Sir Edward Elgar as the song "Roundel: The little eyes that never knew Light".

After the first Poems and Ballads, Swinburne's later poetry was devoted more to philosophy and politics, including the unification of Italy, particularly in the volume Songs before Sunrise. He did not stop writing love poetry entirely, indeed it was only in 1882 that his great epic-length poem, Tristram of Lyonesse, was published, its contents lyrical rather than shocking. His versification, and especially his rhyming technique, remain of high quality to the end.

Algernon Charles Swinburne died of influenza, at the Pines in London on April 10th, 1909 at the age of 72.   He was buried at St. Boniface Church, Bonchurch on the Isle of Wight.

Algernon Charles Swinburne – A Concise Bibliography

Verse Drama
The Queen Mother (1860)
Rosamond (1860)
Chastelard (1865)
Bothwell (1874)
Mary Stuart (1881)
Marino Faliero (1885)
Locrine (1887)
The Sisters (1892)
Rosamund, Queen of the Lombards (1899)

Poetry
Atalanta in Calydon (1865)*
Poems and Ballads (1866)
Songs Before Sunrise (1871)
Songs of Two Nations (1875)
Erechtheus (1876)*

Poems and Ballads, Second Series (1878)
Songs of the Springtides (1880)
Studies in Song (1880)
The Heptalogia, or the Seven against Sense. A Cap with Seven Bells (1880)
Tristram of Lyonesse (1882)
A Dark Month & Other Poems
A Century of Roundels (1883)
A Midsummer Holiday and Other Poems (1884)
Poems and Ballads, Third Series (1889)
Astrophel and Other Poems (1894)
The Tale of Balen (1896)
A Channel Passage and Other Poems (1904)

*Although formally tragedies, Atlanta in Calydon and Erechtheus are traditionally included with his poetry.

Criticism
William Blake: A Critical Essay (1868, new edition 1906)
Under the Microscope (1872)
George Chapman: A Critical Essay (1875)
Essays and Studies (1875)
A Note on Charlotte Brontë (1877)
A Study of Shakespeare (1880)
A Study of Victor Hugo (1886)
A Study of Ben Johnson (1889)
Studies in Prose and Poetry (1894)
The Age of Shakespeare (1908)
Shakespeare (1909)

Major Collections
The Poems of Algernon Charles Swinburne, 6 vols. 1904.
The Tragedies of Algernon Charles Swinburne, 5 vols. 1905.
The Complete Works of Algernon Charles Swinburne, 20 vols. Bonchurch Edition. 1925-7.
The Swinburne Letters, 6 vols. 1959-62.